SUGAR WORK

SUGAR WORK

BLOWN- AND PULLED-SUGAR TECHNIQUES

PETER T. BOYLE

VNR VAN NOSTRAND REINHOLD
_____ New York

Copyright © 1992 by Peter T. Boyle

Library of Congress Catalog Card Number 87-8312

ISBN 0-442-20994-0
ISBN 0-442-01350-7 (paperback)

Printed in the United States of America

Designed by Ann Gold

Van Nostrand Reinhold
115 Fifth Avenue
New York, New York 10003

Chapman and Hall
2-6 Boundary Row
London SE1 8HN, England

Thomas Nelson Australia
102 Dodds Street
South Melbourne 3205
Victoria, Australia

Nelson Canada
1120 Birchmount Road
Scarborough, Ontario MIK 5G4, Canada

16 15 14 13 12 11 10 9 8 7 6 5 4 3 2 1

Library of Congress Cataloging-in-Publication Data

Boyle, Peter T.
    Sugar work

        Includes index.
        1. Sugar art.   2. Confectionery   I. Title.
TX799.B68   1987   641.6'36   87-8312
ISBN 0-442-20994-0
ISBN 0-442-01350-7 (paperback)

SPECIAL THANKS TO

CAL AND JEANIE
BILL AND ELIZABETH

CONTENTS

PREFACE

When I first became interested in the concept of blowing sugar, I searched without success for existing literature covering the topic. In lieu of any substantial written information, I began to research the chemistry of sugar and the science of sugar cooking. Using a traditional recipe as a starting point and relying on the guidance of both academic and industry food chemists, I established a workable general recipe. I further discovered that by altering this recipe I could achieve a more consistent and longlasting finished product, even under the most severe environmental conditions such as high humidity and heat.

I believe sugar blowing and sugar pulling have not become a more prolific part of the American culinary experience for two primary reasons. First is the absence of any definitive information that provides consistent and easily reproducible methods. The other reason is that the art of sugar blowing and sugar pulling requires a considerable amount of time to produce worthwhile results. In the traditional process, sugar must be cooked each time one desires to blow or pull, adding prohibitive labor costs to the finished product. As a result, American hotels, restaurants, and caterers generally have avoided using this costly medium.

I believe I have surmounted both of these difficulties. My process is based on cooking sugar up to forty-five days before it is needed for blowing or pulling. I achieve this longevity by taking the cooked sugar immediately after it has cooled and placing it in small pieces into airtight enclosures along with a new, highly effective desiccant (a moisture-absorbing agent) that sustains a constant 10 percent relative humidity. When sugar is needed for blowing or pulling, it is removed from the airtight storage, warmed to a working temperature under the infrared heat lamps, then colored, aerated, and prepared for blowing or pulling.

If, for example, a chef needs a pulled-sugar flower or a blown-sugar dessert cup for a special restaurant customer, he can remove a piece of stored sugar, and in thirty minutes or less, he has his finished piece. With the traditional method, which demands that sugar be cooked each time one works, the same flower or dessert cup could take two hours or more to complete.

The first part of this book will concentrate on providing a solid foundation in three areas: first, the chemistry and process of sugar cooking; second, a clear understanding of the basic equipment and function of a sugar studio; and third, a presentation of the various new methods and special handling techniques used in this process. The last four parts will concentrate on the production of sugar-blown and sugar-pulled pieces, with a special chapter on candy making.

PART 1
METHODS AND EQUIPMENT

CHAPTER 1

BASIC EQUIPMENT

This chapter illustrates the basic equipment used in sugar work, along with a brief description of the functions of each item. The equipment used in the basic sugar studio (four-bulb heating system, standard blowpipe set, fabric work rack, hot-wire cutter) was designed by me specifically for this process.

COOKING AND STORING PROCESS

The equipment described below is illustrated in figure 1–1.

SAUCEPAN (A)

A Cuisinart stainless steel saucepan is recommended for cooking sugar. The innovative design of the lip of this saucepan prevents hot sugar from flowing down the outside of the saucepan while pouring. The saucepan's specially constructed heat-conductive bottom allows the sugar to cook quickly and uniformly.

CANDY THERMOMETER (B)

A candy thermometer is used to gauge the temperature of the syrup during the cooking process. A stainless steel candy thermometer that fastens to the inside of the saucepan is recommended, although any accurate and easily readable thermometer can be substituted.

Changes in barometric pressure and the location's relationship to sea level will affect the performance of a candy thermometer. To find a true reading each day you cook sugar, boil water for five minutes with the thermometer in place. If the water boils at 209°F, subtract three degrees from the final cooking temperature of the sugar. Conversely, water boiling at 215°F will require three degrees added to the final cooking temperature.

PASTRY BRUSH (C)

A natural bristle pastry brush is used to remove the droplets of syrup that escape from the batch surface in the early stages of the cooking process and adhere to the lip and inside wall of the saucepan. A natural bristle paintbrush is an acceptable substitute for a pastry brush, but do not use dyed natural bristle (gold, brown, black) and never use a synthetic bristle brush.

STAINLESS STEEL STRAINER (D)

A stainless steel strainer is used to remove the residue of mineral salts that appear on the batch surface at the onset of rapid boil. Never use steel strainers because of their potential for corrosion. Even one rust particle will contaminate and crystallize the sugar batch.

EYEDROPPER (E)

A small glass eyedropper is used to add the tartaric acid and water mixture to the syrup in the final

1-1. The equipment for cooking, pouring, and storing process (see text for label explanations).

stages of the cooking process. The eyedropper is available in most drugstores. Do not use the larger plastic eyedroppers.

RUBBER SPATULA (F)

A rubber spatula is used to stir the sugar and boiling water into a transparent sucrose solution prior to the cooking process. Using a rubber spatula to stir the mixture will alert you tactilely to the presence of undissolved sugar crystals.

MARBLE SLAB (G)

After the cooking process, the hot sugar is poured onto a lightly oiled marble slab. Any vegetable oil can be used. The marble slab absorbs the heat and allows the sugar to cool slowly and uniformly, while the oil prevents it from sticking to the surface.

Tight-seamed white marble with or without thin gray veins is recommended for this process. The marble must be at least ½ inch thick; the thicker the marble, the better its ability to absorb the heat.

METAL SPATULA (H)

A metal spatula is used to remove the sugar from the marble slab. The edge of the metal spatula also can be used to score the surface of the hot sugar lightly right after the sugar has been poured onto the marble slab. After it cools the sugar can be easily separated at the scoreline into smaller pieces.

COOLING RACK (I)

When the sugar solidifies, it is removed from the marble and placed on a wire cooling rack until completely cooled.

METAL MOLDS—SUGAR POURING (J)

Assorted shapes of metal molds are used to create solid sugar bases, which serve as the foundations for sugar centerpieces or as the bottoms for blown-sugar wine glasses, dessert cups, and other functional pieces.

The circular copper molds illustrated here were made by cutting 2- and 3-inch-diameter copper pipes into 1-inch-long strips. The detailed molds were fabricated using galvanized sheet metal and stainless steel.

Some of the heavier metal cookie-cutter and flan molds can also be used as poured-sugar molds. Additionally, most commercial sculpting clays can be used as mold materials. Sculpting clay is spread at least 1 inch thick on the marble, and a silhouette of the desired shape is then cut out. Also, strips of clay 1 inch thick and 1 inch wide can be used to create an outline.

HUMI-SORB AND INDICATOR CARDS (K)

This process allows precooked sugar to be stored for up to six weeks. This longevity is achieved by storing the precooked sugar in airtight enclosures with a desiccant called Humi-sorb. A desiccant is a moisture-absorbing agent used to remove moisture from the air.

Humi-sorb is a highly efficient clay desiccant that is packaged in dust-resistant 1-ounce bags. It is chemically inert, odorless, tasteless, nontoxic, and noncorrosive. It is also considerably lower in cost than silica gel desiccants, as well as being superior in performance at the lower relative humidity ranges. Humi-sorb can reduce and maintain a 10 percent relative humidity within an airtight enclosure.

An indicator card is used to measure the relative humidity within the airtight enclosure. When activated, the card displays three blue circles, each circle representing a different level of relative humidity (10, 15, or 20 percent). As the humidity rises within the enclosure, the blue circles turn pink as the respective level of relative humidity is reached.

For the best results, the stored sugar should be maintained at or below 10 percent relative humidity. When the humidity rises above 10 percent, the Humi-sorb should be replaced. Humi-sorb can be reactivated and reused for up to four years. To reactivate, place the bag(s) of Humi-sorb on a rack in an oven set at 250°F for sixteen hours; it is then ready for reuse. If the Humi-sorb is handled carefully, it can be used for months without having to reactivate.

FIBERGLASS SCREENING (L)

A tight-meshed fiberglass screening is used to wrap and separate pieces of precooked sugar during storage. This inert material was selected because it does not stick to the sugar and can be reused indefinitely.

Gray or black fiberglass screening is used conventionally in house windows as a substitute for metal screening. It is inexpensive and can be purchased in most hardware stores.

AIRTIGHT ENCLOSURE (M)

Any container that can be rendered airtight can be used to store precooked sugar. Clear plastic freezer storage bags with zipperlike seals work well, as do plastic refrigerator containers or 5-gallon plastic pails with lids.

BASIC SUGAR-STUDIO EQUIPMENT

The equipment described on the next few pages is illustrated in figure 1–2.

1-2. The basic sugar studio equipment (see text for label explanations).

FOUR-BULB HEATING SYSTEM (A)

The bulbs in the four-bulb heating system are standard 250-watt infrared bulbs. The bulbs can be made of either white or red glass. Each bulb is controlled by a light dimmer, which is attached on the cord. The four-bulb heating system was designed to supply heat to soften the precooked sugar for blowing and pulling and to maintain the sugar's working temperature safely while work is being performed. The design of the four-bulb heating system was perfected based on years of experience. Although even a single-bulb system can successfully produce finished pieces, I prefer the four-bulb heating system because of its capacity to work with large volumes of sugar, as well as its ability to produce results quickly. The four-bulb heating system can be made, or it can be purchased.

Note: The working times in the preparation and production chapters have been calculated using the four-bulb heating system.

FABRIC WORK RACK (B)

The fabric work rack serves as the working surface
for the four-bulb heating system. It is also the best
surface for safely storing pulled or blown pieces until
they are assembled into a centerpiece. The white fabric is 100 percent polyester and has a nonsheen texture. It is stretched tightly and stapled over the top
of a wooden frame, which provides a firm work surface. The frame is 24 inches long by 24 inches wide,
and is made of an inexpensive wood, like pine. If
carefully maintained, the fabric can withstand at
least one year of weekly use.

Note: Never push down hard on the fabric work surface. If a firm surface is desired, use the top of the
wooden frame around the perimeter of the rack.

    In a large sink or shower, rinse the racks with hot
water and towel dry the entire rack after each work
day. A mild detergent can be used when necessary,
but be sure to rinse the rack thoroughly before reusing. Both the wooden frame and the fabric must be
completely dry before the rack can be reused.

STANDARD BLOWPIPE SET (C)

The standard blowpipe set (fig. 1–3) consists of
eight Pyrex glass sugar-blowing tubes and tools, six
blowpipes ranging from 6 to 22 millimeters in diameter, and two solid glass manipulators used to apply
food coloring and make various manipulations on the
sugar. The choice of blowpipe is determined by the
size of the piece of sugar being blown. As the piece
of sugar increases in size, so should the diameter of
the blowpipe (fig. 1–4). The 8-millimeter blowpipe
can be blown from either end, but the 10-, 14-, 18-,
and 22-millimeter blowpipes have tapered ends that
are used as the mouthpiece.

    At the end of the work day, the best method for
cleaning the blowpipe is to place the pipe in boiling
water until all the sugar is removed. The blowpipe
must be completely dry before reusing. Even a slight
residue of moisture left on the inside of the pipe can
cause the sugar to crystallize. While you are working, the blowpipe can be cleaned for quick reuse by
rotating the end of the pipe over the flame of an

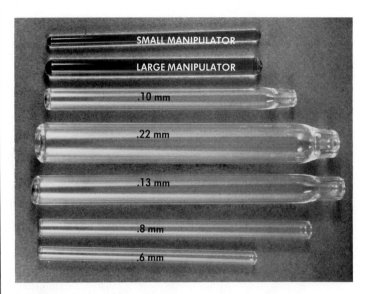

1-3. The standard blowpipe set.

1–4. STANDARD BLOWPIPE SET

SIZE	NUMBER	COMMON USAGE	MAXIMUM-DIAMETER SPHERE
8 mm	2 pieces	Grape, strawberry, Easter egg	3 inches
10 mm	1 piece	Banana, lemon, dolphin, small Christmas ornament	4 inches
13 mm	1 piece	Orange, candy dish, Christmas ornament	6 inches
18 mm	1 piece	Pineapple, bud vase, medium swan	8 inches
22 mm	1 piece	Wine glass, large vase, large swan	12 inches
Small rod (solid glass)	1 piece	Used to apply food color	
Large rod (solid glass)	1 piece	Making the initial airchamber prior to inserting blowpipe	

alcohol burner and using a small knife to scrape the warm sugar from the blowpipe.

Note: I developed the eight-piece blowpipe set after years of experience as a glassblower and sugarblower. The set provides a good range of sizes necessary to create a wide selection of sugar-blown pieces. The sturdy Pyrex blowpipes have a melting temperature of 1100°F, which makes them impervious to overheating under normal conditions.

ALCOHOL BURNER (D)

The alcohol burner uses methyl alcohol or denatured alcohol to produce a clean, carbonless flame. The primary purpose of the alcohol burner is to supply the heating source required to weld sugar. The alcohol burner also is used to warm the blowpipe prior to the blowing process and as the alternative method of

removing the blowpipe from a finished piece; these processes are described in Chapter 5.

SCISSORS (E)

A pair of stainless steel scissors is used to cut and trim hot sugar throughout the process. Before the scissors can be used, the sugar must be uniformly heated, or the scissors will produce crystals in the sugar.

PASTE FOOD COLORING (F)

Paste food coloring is used for coloring the sugar in this process of sugar work. The pastes are concentrated and require very small amounts to produce their colors. In my experience, the various manufacturers of paste food coloring vary in the number of colors they offer, but the quality is very similar. Do not use liquid food coloring, and only use semiliquid food coloring during the cooking process.

HOT-WIRE CUTTER (G)

The hot-wire cutter has a "step down" transformer that lowers electrical current, which heats the nickel-chromium wire to red hot. The hot-wire cutter was designed to split a blown-sugar sphere in half by passing it through the hot wire, making both halves a potential dessert cup, candy dish, wine glass, or other functional object. The hot-wire cutter also has proven to be the most efficient method of removing the blowpipe from a finished sugar-blown piece.

FAN (H)

A fan is used to cool pieces of blown and pulled sugar immediately after they are completed. Unless otherwise stated, the fan is set on high when it is used. Any style or size of fan can be used, although the larger the fan, the shorter the cooling time.

PLASTIC BELL MOLD (I)

The plastic bell is used as a mold to blow a sugar wine glass vessel.

CHAPTER 2

SUGAR COOKING, POURING, AND STORING PROCEDURES

The most important aspect of sugar work is the sugar cooking process. Consistent and long-lasting results in sugar work require: a precise measurement of the ingredients; an exact calculation of the environmental conditions and the final cooking temperature; your full attention during the sugar cooking, cooling, and storing procedures. Without this care, the sugar will not perform up to its full capacity; when little care is used, the sugar will not perform at all.

INGREDIENTS

The ingredients used in the cooking process are: pure cane sugar, distilled water, corn syrup, and tartaric acid. Oil-base flavoring or food coloring also may be added when flavored or one-color sugar is desired.

PURE CANE SUGAR
Most of the pure cane sugars on the market today are at least 99.8 percent pure sucrose. The remaining components are naturally occurring mineral salts such as calcium and carbonate, which are not removed during the refining process, in order to keep sugar at its reasonable price. Pure sucrose would be very expensive.

Large amounts of naturally occurring mineral salts can have an adverse effect on sugar during the cooking process. These mineral salts discolor and give the cooked sugar an increased amber color. This color

negatively affects the coloring process described in chapter 3: reds turn orange, for example, and blues turn green. A substantial quantity of mineral salts present during the cooking process can also cause the sugar molecules to bond with the salt molecules: this bonding causes the sugar to crystallize.

In my experimentation, I have found the various brands of pure cane sugar to vary slightly in their mineral salt content. California and Hawaii (C&H) and Dixie pure cane sugars, in my experience, were found to have the least amount of these mineral salts. I recommend you experiment with the pure cane sugars available in your area to measure the mineral salt content. The mineral salts appear as a film on the surface of the batch prior to rapid boil and are easily removed using a small strainer (see *Cooking Process* in this chapter).

DISTILLED WATER
Distilled water is used to reduce the sucrose crystals (cane sugar) into a syrup without burning or discoloring the sugar. It is used in place of tap water to avoid large quantities of minerals sometimes found in tap water especially in cities.

CORN SYRUP
Corn syrup is used because it inhibits crystallization by impeding the motion of sugar and water molecules, which makes it more difficult for the sucrose to return to its crystalline state. Corn syrup gives the

sugar a flexibility that allows it to be pulled and blown without the sugar snapping or breaking apart. Although most corn syrups on the market will provide reasonable results, I have found that a 44 Baumé corn syrup, such as Staley 4400 Sweetose, is one of the best for this type of sugar work.

TARTARIC ACID

Crystallization also can be impeded by adding a small amount of tartaric acid to the sugar. In the presence of acid and heat, sucrose is inverted, or broken down into its two components: glucose and fructose. The tartaric acid also gives the sugar flexibility. The tartaric acid is mixed with distilled water using a ratio of 1 part (teaspoon) tartaric acid to 6 parts (teaspoons) distilled water.

THE BASIC RECIPE

This recipe uses weighed measurements. A 5-pound portion scale is used in this process, although any accurate scale can be used. The ingredient ratio is 10 parts cane sugar, 6 parts distilled water, and 1½ parts corn syrup. One drop of tartaric acid is added for every 10 ounces of sugar. The recipe can be increased or decreased as long as this ratio is maintained. This recipe is the basic sugar-boiling recipe:

> 80 ounces cane sugar
> 48 ounces distilled water
> 12 ounces corn syrup
> 8 drops tartaric acid
>
> 300°F—final cooking temperature

The final cooking temperature and the ingredients must be altered to compensate for increases in air temperature, relative humidity, or when larger blown-sugar pieces are attempted. Corn syrup and tartaric acid give the sugar a flexibility that allows it to be stretched, pulled, and blown without cracking or breaking apart. As the air temperature and relative humidity increase, or when blowing a large-sized piece, the basic recipe must be altered to make the sugar less flexible and soft, which often causes

the sugar to collapse soon after the piece is finished. Increasing the final cooking temperature, while decreasing the amounts of corn syrup and tartaric acid, makes the sugar stronger-walled and less susceptible to collapse. The basic recipe is used when the air temperature is 75°F or lower and the relative humidity is 50 percent or lower. Under these environmental conditions, the basic recipe can be used for all sizes of pulled sugar and blown sugar not larger than a 10-inch-diameter sphere or its equivalent.

RECIPE ALTERATIONS, FINAL COOKING TEMPERATURE

For every Fahrenheit increase of ten degrees in the air temperature above 75°F, add two degrees to the final cooking temperature. For every 10 percent increase in the relative humidity higher than 50 percent, add two degrees to the final cooking temperature. Round off the air temperature to the nearest ten degrees Fahrenheit and the relative humidity to the nearest 10 percent.

For blown-sugar pieces larger than a 10-inch-diameter sphere or its equivalent, add one degree Fahrenheit for every two-inch increase in diameter. Round off the increase in diameter to the nearest two inches. Regardless of the size of the blown-sugar piece or the severity of the environmental conditions, never cook the sugar above 318°F. When the sugar is cooked above this temperature, it becomes brittle and extremely difficult to work. When the air temperature and the relative humidity are high, extra large pieces of blown sugar should not be attempted.

Pulled sugar requires an increase in the final cooking temperature when the environmental conditions warrant, but does not require an increase when large pieces are attempted.

EXAMPLES

When the air temperature is 93°F and the relative humidity is 76 percent, the final cooking temperature is 310°F. This sugar can be used for all pulled sugar and blown sugar not larger than a 10-inch-diameter sphere or its equivalent.

When blowing a 14-inch-diameter sphere or its

equivalent, with the air temperature at 82°F and the relative humidity at 66 percent, the final cooking temperature is 308°F.

When blowing a 28-inch-diameter sphere or its equivalent, with the air temperature at 95°F and the relative humidity at 88 percent, the final cooking temperature is 320°F, which is two degrees above the maximum recommended final cooking temperature. A piece of this size only should be attempted when the combined air temperature and relative humidity add just ten degrees Fahrenheit to the final cooking temperature.

RECIPE ALTERATIONS, INGREDIENTS

For every twenty degree Fahrenheit increase in the air temperature above 75°F, decrease 1 ounce of corn syrup and 1 drop of tartaric acid from the basic recipe. For every 20 percent increase in relative humidity above 50 percent, decrease 1 ounce of corn syrup and 1 drop of tartaric acid from the basic recipe. Round off the air temperature to the nearest twenty degrees Fahrenheit and the relative humidity to the nearest 20 percent.

Blown-sugar pieces larger than a 10-inch-diameter sphere or its equivalent should decrease 1 ounce of corn syrup and 1 drop of tartaric acid for every six-inch increase in diameter. Round off the increase in diameter to the nearest six inches. Regardless of size of the blown-sugar piece or the severity of the environmental conditions, never decrease more than 4 ounces of corn syrup or 4 drops of tartaric acid from the basic recipe.

Pulled sugar requires a reduction of ingredients as the environmental conditions warrant, but does not require a reduction of the ingredients when larger pieces are attempted.

EXAMPLES

When the air temperature is 93°F and the relative humidity is 76 percent, decrease 2 ounces of corn syrup and 2 drops of tartaric acid from the basic recipe. This sugar can be used for all pulled sugar and blown sugar not larger than a 10-inch diameter.

When blowing a 14-inch-diameter sphere or its equivalent, with the air temperature at 82°F and the

relative humidity at 66 percent, decrease 2 ounces of corn syrup and 2 drops of tartaric acid from the basic recipe.

When blowing a 20-inch-diameter sphere or its equivalent, with the air temperature at 95°F and the relative humidity at 88 percent, the conditions warrant a decrease of 5 ounces of corn syrup and 5 drops of tartaric acid, which is more than the maximum recommended ingredient reduction. A piece this size only should be attempted when the air temperature and the relative humidity combined require just 2 ounces of corn syrup and 2 drops of tartaric acid to be decreased from the basic recipe.

Note: Under most environmental conditions, small pieces of pulled and blown sugar can be made using the basic recipe or any of the altered recipes. As the environmental conditions turn severe, the recipe must be altered to accomplish consistent results. The recipe alterations allow you to achieve an optimum performance from the sugar under all environmental conditions.

For the best results, always be prepared to work under all types of environmental conditions. I do this by cooking and storing several batches of sugar using a wide range of altered recipes that anticipate both larger-sized blown sugar as well as the entire scope of environmental conditions.

COOKING PROCESS PREPARATION

All the equipment, utensils, and ingredients required for the cooking process should be assembled and prepared before the cooking process begins (see chapter 1).

1. In separate containers, weigh out the appropriate amounts of cane sugar, distilled water, and corn syrup.

2. In a small container, mix 1 teaspoon of tartaric acid with 6 teaspoons of distilled water.

3. Fill a small bowl with distilled water, which is used to wet the natural bristle brush.

4. Fill a large bowl with ice and then add tap water until the bowl is four-fifths full. The ice water is used to arrest the cooking process after the sugar has reached the final cooking temperature.

5. Place the unoiled marble on a tabletop away from the cooking area, positioned for easy pouring, and place the wire cooling rack close to the marble.

6. Position all the utensils near the working area and make certain that the utensils or equipment that come into contact with the sugar are impeccably clean!

REDUCING THE SUGAR

The sugar is reduced by mixing it with boiling water and stirring with a rubber spatula until all the sugar grains dissolve to create a clear syrup. Using a rubber spatula will allow you to feel any undissolved grains of sugar present in the syrup. Since a single grain of undissolved sugar at the start of the cooking process can cause an entire batch of sugar to crystallize, reducing the sugar thoroughly before it is cooked guarantees a crystalfree batch.

Using the amounts from the recipe, bring the distilled water to a boil. Turn the heat off and slowly add the sugar while stirring the mixture. Continue to stir for approximately 2 minutes or until the batch is clear. A few crystals remain on the bottom of the saucepan after the initial stirring, but stirring twice more over a 10-minute period will dissolve all the crystals. After the sugar is reduced, the syrup can be cooked immediately or it can be sealed in an airtight container and stored at room temperature for up to 1 week. Before reusing, the container of syrup is immersed in a large bowl of hot water for approximately 10 minutes. When the syrup is warm, stir vigorously before using.

COOKING PROCESS

Slight caramelization occurs when sugar is cooked at high temperatures. The faster the sugar reaches its final cooking temperature, the less caramelization will occur. A gas range is recommended for cooking the sugar. Propane burns approximately 30 percent hotter than natural gas, so a propane range is more desirable than a natural gas range, although not mandatory. An electric range cooks sugar much slower than propane or natural gas ranges and is not recommended. I usually use a propane camping stove to cook sugar.

1. Pour the sugar syrup into a saucepan and place it uncovered on top of the gas range. Turn the flame on high, but do not allow the flame to extend beyond the bottom perimeter of the saucepan, and be sure the saucepan is centrally located over the flame.

2. As the sugar syrup approaches the boiling point, a thin residue appears across the batch surface. The residue contains small amounts of naturally occurring mineral salts such as calcium and carbonate that are not completely removed during the refining process. At the onset of rapid boil, the residue collects together at the center of the batch surface. Using a small stainless steel strainer, remove the residue (fig. 2–1).

3. From the start of rapid boil until the sugar reaches 240°F, droplets of dissolved sugar and water escape from the surface of the sugar syrup and stick on the lip and insides of the saucepan. The water from the droplet quickly evaporates, leaving a sugar grain that will fall into the batch and cause it to crystallize if left unattended.

Using a moist natural bristle brush, remove the grains from the lip and insides of the saucepan (fig. 2–2). Continue to brush every two minutes until the droplets stop escaping from the batch. Before each brushing, dip the brush into a bowl of distilled water and squeeze the bristles to remove the excess water. At the start of rapid boil, hundreds of droplets scatter from the surface of the sugar syrup. By the time the temperature of the sugar syrup reaches 230°F, only a few droplets continue to escape, and at 235°F, the droplets cease to escape.

Note: If the saucepan is covered with a lid from the start of rapid boil to 235°F, steam from within the saucepan will remove the majority of the sugar grains. When the lid is lifted, the lip and the insides of the saucepan should be brushed to remove all the grains. Before using a lid, time at least two batches of the sugar syrup to calculate exactly how long it takes to reach 235°F from rapid boil. The thermometer is placed in the saucepan at 235°F, as soon as the droplets have stopped escaping from the batch. Using a stainless steel saucepan with a copper bottom on a propane gas range, the basic recipe takes approximately 20 minutes to go from rapid boil to 235°F.

4. Add the appropriate amount of corn syrup to the center of the batch, but do not stir (fig. 2–3). The boiling action quickly blends the corn syrup into the sugar syrup. The corn syrup can be added safely at any temperature between 232°F and 242°F. I usually add the corn syrup at 242°F.

5. At 270°F, stir the small container of tartaric acid and distilled water to make sure they are blended thoroughly. At 280°F, use an eyedropper to add the appropriate number of drops. Add the drops by evenly placing them across the surface of the batch (fig. 2–4).

    If colored or flavored sugar is desired, both coloring and flavor can be added at 280°F. Carefully add the flavoring by using an eyedropper. Only oil-based flavorings should be used. The paste food coloring is added by using either the small solid glass manipulator (see *Standard Blowpipe Set* in chapter 1) or a toothpick.

6. At 300°F or at the appropriate final cooking temperature, stop the cooking process by immersing the bottom of the saucepan into a large bowl of ice water for approximately 3 seconds. After the saucepan is removed from the ice water, watch the thermometer for 30 seconds. If the temperature continues to rise, return the saucepan to the ice water until the temperature stabilizes. Place the saucepan on top of the range with the flame

2-1. Remove the residue from the batch surface.

2-2. Brush the sides of the pan with a damp brush.

2-3. Add the corn syrup at the center of the batch surface.

2-4. Evenly place the drops of acid across the surface of the batch.

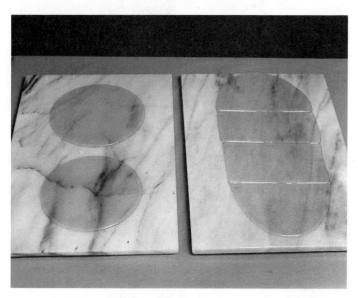

2-5. The two basic pouring shapes.

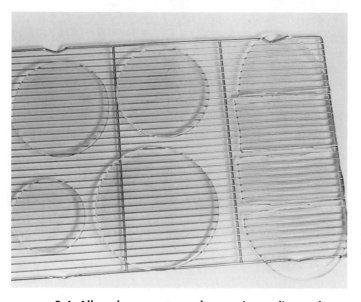

2-6. Allow the sugar to cool on a wire cooling rack.

turned off and let the batch stand until the majority of the air bubbles in the syrup disappear, which occurs at approximately 280°F. The syrup continues to cook after it is removed from the flame. If the cooking process is not stopped, the temperature of the syrup can rise as much as ten degrees over the intended final cooking temperature.

While the batch cools, lightly oil the marble slab and the rubber and metal spatulas.

7. Remove the thermometer carefully and wipe the bottom of the saucepan with a damp cloth to remove any carbon that may have accumulated during the cooking process. The sugar syrup is now ready to be poured onto the marble.

POURING PROCEDURES

The hot sugar is poured onto the marble into two basic shapes. One shape is a long narrow slab and the other is a circular disk (fig. 2–5). Hold the saucepan close to the marble, while slowly and evenly pouring the sugar onto the marble. Use an oiled spatula to wipe the edge of the saucepan after each pour. Do not allow the threads of sugar that extend from the edge of the saucepan to return to the batch.

SLAB

Always pour uniform slabs. This is best accomplished by pouring slowly and steadily. Before the sugar solidifies, the edge of an oiled metal spatula is used to lightly score the slab shortly after it has been poured onto the marble (fig. 2–5). The scorelines should divide the slab into equal pieces. After the sugar has solidified, carefully remove it from the marble using an oiled spatula and set it on a wire cooling rack (fig. 2–6). After the sugar has cooled, it is easily separated at the scores. Always score the slab at an even depth not more than 1/16 inch. When the slab is scored at an uneven depth, the sugar is very hard to separate and usually shatters.

The pieces separated from the slab are rough and very fragile along the edge that has been separated. If these pieces are stored for later use, extreme care should be taken while packing them for storage. I use these in my sugar-work seminars because they provide both the small-sized pieces and the amount of pieces required to teach large groups; however, because of their fragility, I never store pieces from the slab for my own work.

CIRCULAR DISK

A circular disk is made by pouring slowly and steadily in one spot on the marble until the desired size circle is reached. The circular disks are the starting shapes for the preparations discussed in this book. The edges of the circular disks are smooth, which makes the disks less fragile and better for storage than pieces from the slab.

After the sugar has solidified, carefully remove it from the marble using an oiled metal spatula and set it on a wire cooling rack (fig. 2–6). When the sugar has completely cooled, it can be used immediately or it can be stored for later use.

Plastic storage bags (see *Airtight Enclosure* in chapter 1) can accommodate circular disks up to 10 inches in diameter. Subsequent chapters in this book use circular disks between 5 and 10 inches in diameter.

STORING PROCEDURES

Sugar is very hygroscopic, which means it readily absorbs atmospheric moisture. If the sugar is exposed to high levels of moisture for extended periods, it will begin to crystallize. Precooked sugar, as well as finished sugar pieces, must be stored in air-tight enclosures with moisture-absorbing agents.

PRECOOKED SUGAR

Plastic freezer bags are used as the airtight enclosure for storing precooked sugar. Strips of fiberglass screening, 12 inches wide and 36 inches long, are used to separate pieces of precooked sugar while they are being stored. A piece of sugar is placed on the screen at one end of the strip and, together, the sugar and the screen are folded once toward the opposite end. The screen covers the piece of sugar as it is folded. Another piece of sugar is placed on top

of the first and this procedure is continued until the screen cannot accommodate any more pieces (fig. 2–7). The sugar is then put into the freezer bag and packets of Humi-sorb are added along with an indicator card that is used to measure the relative humidity within the bag (see *Humi-sorb and Indicator Cards* in chapter 1). I usually add eight 1-ounce packets of Humi-sorb and one indicator card in each freezer bag of stored sugar. After the bag is sealed, it is placed into another bag for added protection. For the best results, always store the precooked sugar at 10 percent relative humidity or lower.

Precooked sugar can be stored for up to 6 weeks. Several of my students claim that they have achieved even greater longevity. Some have successfully used sugar that has been stored for over 3 months. To guarantee a long storing life, periodically check the indicator cards in the bags. If the moisture rises above 10 percent relative humidity, replace the Humi-sorb with reactivated Humi-sorb.

Note: The sugar must be cooled completely before storing. Even a trace of warmth in the sugar can cause the pieces to stick through the fiberglass screen. Never allow the pieces of sugar to touch while in storage. Any type of airtight enclosure can be used.

FINISHED PIECES

Finished blown- and pulled-sugar centerpieces can be kept indefinitely when stored in an airtight container, such as a plexiglass box, at 10 percent relative humidity or less. The plexiglass box should have a false bottom with an open air way to the top of the box. The false bottom is used to store the Humi-sorb. Gradually add packets of Humi-sorb into the false bottom until an indicator card inside of the box indicates the relative humidity is below 10 percent.

POURED-SUGAR BASES

Poured-sugar bases are used as the foundations for all the centerpieces in this book. The bases are created by pouring hot sugar into metal molds placed on the

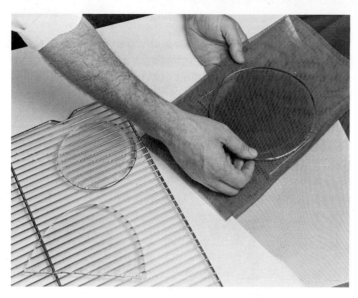

2-7. Wrap the sugar into the fiberglass screening.

marble. The marble and the insides of the metal molds must be oiled lightly before pouring.

Multipiece metal molds can be fashioned to create a poured-sugar centerpiece, such as a house, a crown, or a stained glass window. After all the parts of the poured-sugar centerpiece have been poured and cooled, they are assembled using the bonding procedures described in chapter 4.

Poured sugar uses the same cooking procedures as the standard cooking process, but the recipe must be altered when large pieces are desired. The basic recipe can be used to make poured-sugar bases 6 inches in diameter or smaller. Poured-sugar bases larger than 6 inches in diameter should decrease 1 drop of tartaric acid for every 3-inch increase in the diameter, up to a maximum of 5 drops. The bases are colored by adding food coloring to the syrup at 280°F.

SMALL BASE

A poured-sugar base 6 inches in diameter or smaller is made by pouring the hot sugar into the center of the mold and allowing the sugar to spread to the edges (fig. 2–8). I usually pour my small bases ¼ inch thick.

A star-shaped metal mold 3 inches in diameter and 1 inch high is used to create the bottom of the wine glass in chapter 13. The bottom is made by pouring sugar into the center of the mold until the sugar is ¼ inch thick.

LARGE BASE

A poured-sugar base larger than 6 inches in diameter is made by pouring the sugar at one end of the mold and zigzagging the pour from side to side until you reach the other end (fig. 2–9). Never pour the sugar close to the sides of the mold. Pour at least 1 inch away from the sides and allow the sugar to spread to the edges. I generally pour a 10-inch-diameter base or its equivalent, ½ inch thick, and a 20-inch-diameter base or its equivalent, ¾ inch thick.

ATTACHING SUGAR TO BASES

Small pieces of pulled and blown sugar, such as the bud vase (chapter 8), the dessert cups (chapter 11), and the candy dishes (chapter 12), are attached to the base by heating a small area at the center of the base over the flame of an alcohol burner until small clear bubbles appear on its surface. The piece of sugar is set in place and pulled away slightly from the base immediately after it is attached to create a strong and permanent bond.

Larger pieces, such as some of the pulled-sugar wave-strips (chapter 7), the large vase (chapter 8), the swan (chapter 9), and the large fruit bowl (chapter 6), require both the base and the piece to be heated to the small, clear bubble stage before attaching. The ends of the two pieces of pulled-sugar wave containing the wires are heated along with the base before each piece is attached. A small piece of sugar is attached to the bottom of large pieces of blown sugar and then this small piece, along with the base, are heated to the small, clear bubble stage and attached. After a large piece is attached, it also should be pulled away slightly from the base immediately after attaching to create a strong and permanent bond.

THICK BASE

A thick poured-sugar base 3 inches in diameter and 7/8 inch thick is used to blow a wine glass vessel in chapter 13. A circular metal mold, 3 inches in diameter and 1 inch high is used to create the base made by pouring sugar into the center of the mold until the sugar is 1/8 inch from the top edge of the mold.

The thick base uses the same cooking procedures as the standard cooking process. The sugar is colored by adding food coloring to the syrup at 280°F (see step 5 of *Cooking Process*).

2-8. Pour the sugar at the center of the small mold.

2-9. Using a zigzag pattern, pour the sugar into the large mold, going from one end to the other. Pour at least 1 inch away from the sides.

CHAPTER 3

PREPARATION OF PRECOOKED SUGAR

The most important elements in this method of sugar work are the ability to store precooked sugar until it is needed and the ability to transform the precooked sugar back into a working state. This chapter will supply the techniques required to reheat the precooked sugar for the aeration, blowing, and pulling processes.

Circular disks of precooked sugar are used here as the starting shape. Although circular disks are the most suitable shape for storage, the starting shape is arbitrary and circular disks were selected for the purpose of maintaining continuity in the book.

INITIAL REHEATING

Place an 8-inch-diameter disk of precooked sugar at the center of the fabric work rack. Using a four-bulb heating system, turn the bulbs on to their highest dimmer switch setting. While carefully bending the gooseneck-stem lamps, adjust the beams of the infrared bulbs onto the sugar until the light completely covers the sugar's surface. Make certain the sugar is completely within the aura being projected onto the fabric work rack (fig. 3–1). In order to maintain a uniform temperature, always keep the sugar within the light aura during the reheating process. To prevent serious burns, do not handle either the porcelain sockets or the infrared bulbs when adjusting the bulbs' beam.

The distance between the sugar and the infrared bulbs is less important than always maintaining the sugar within the light aura. The distance between the sugar and the bulbs increases as the volume of sugar becomes larger.

Heat the sugar disk until it is very pliable; when lifted from the fabric work rack it should sag in your hand. When the sugar is supple, turn it over on the fabric work rack. If excessive wrinkles and small stress cracks appear on the sugar's surface when lifted, continued heating is necessary. Using a four-bulb heating system, it will take approximately 4 minutes to fully heat the top side of the sugar disk.

ADDING COLOR

Heat the reverse side of the sugar disk until a high-gloss shine starts to appear on the sugar's surface. This takes approximately 2 minutes. Using the small solid-glass manipulator or a toothpick, add a drop of paste food coloring at the center of the sugar disk (fig. 3–2). Continue to heat the sugar until the high-gloss shine completely covers the sugar's surface. Fold the sugar disk in half being careful not to trap any air bubbles while folding. Adjust the rounded edges of the semicircle to create the rectangular building shape (fig. 3–3). The color spreads uniformly throughout the sugar during the aeration process.

Using a four-bulb heating system, it will take approximately 3 minutes to sufficiently heat the

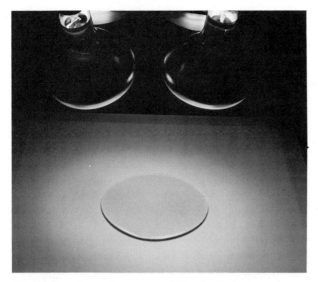
3-1. Always keep the sugar within the light aura.

3-2. Add the food coloring at the center of the sugar.

reverse side of the sugar disk. A pure white sugar is attained without adding any food coloring. The white color is accomplished by aerating the sugar until it is fully opaque.

RECTANGULAR BUILDING SHAPE

A rectangle of uniform thickness, approximately two times longer than it is wide, is always the required starting and working shape when building the sugar, regardless of the volume of sugar.

BUILDING THE SUGAR

The term *building the sugar* refers to the procedure used to heat the sugar to a working temperature. In this process, hot surface sugar is folded repeatedly into its center. This brings the cooler sugar to the surface. The hot sugar trapped in the center supplies an internal heating source, which in combination with the external heating source (infrared bulbs), provides an efficient means of heating the sugar to a working temperature.

Heat the sugar until the high-gloss shine completely covers its surface. Lengthen the rectangle by pulling out both ends evenly to half the length of the original rectangle, and in the same motion, fold the ends back to the center (fig. 3–4). Do not trap any

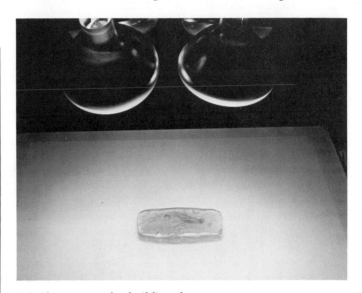
3-3. The rectangular building shape.

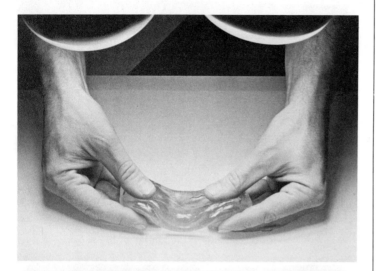

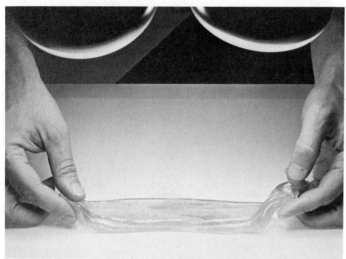

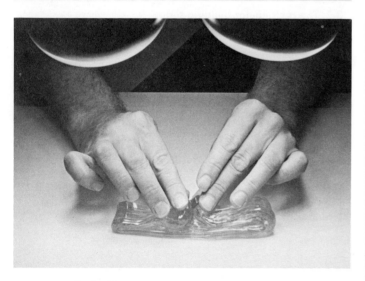

3-4. The building process.

air bubbles while folding the sugar. To avoid this, always fold the ends back to the center carefully and gradually. The ends should meet flush at the center of the rectangle and should never overlap. Always maintain the rectangular building shape as well as a uniform thickness in the sugar throughout the building process. Repeat the building procedure until the sugar has reached the working temperature, approximately 175°F. The sugar is very fluid at this temperature and has the consistency of hot wax or hot taffy during a taffy-pull. Using a four-bulb system, I generally build an 8-inch disk of sugar four times before it reaches the working temperature.

Note: Always wait for a uniform high-gloss shine to cover the sugar's surface completely before building the sugar. Never heat the sugar beyond the high-gloss shine. If the sugar is overheated, tiny bubbles appear on the surface that can cause the sugar to crystallize.

AERATING THE SUGAR

Aeration is the procedure used to circulate air through the sugar by pulling and twisting the hot sugar manually. Molecules of air and sugar combine to form a framework similar to the infrastructure of a beehive. The air molecules are similar to the hive's honeycomb walls and the sugar symbolizes the hive cells. This sturdy arrangement of molecules lines up into thin bands that run throughout the sugar. The result of this molecular configuration supplies the sugar with a backbone that allows it to be blown into extremely thin-walled ornaments or pulled into paper-thin petals that retain their shape after they have cooled.

The sugar is transparent as the aeration begins. As the sugar is pulled and twisted, it changes to a translucent state and then to an opaque one, which is the final aeration phase. The sugar cannot be aerated past the opaque stage without causing crystallization.

In my experience, when the sugar is aerated to a total opacity, it exhibits its greatest strength and capacity to be blown or pulled into a very large and thin finished piece. After it has been heated to the correct working temperature, sugar can be blown or pulled in a transparent or translucent state, but in order to maintain the same wall strength, transparent and translucent finished pieces must be at least twice the wall thickness of an opaque finished piece. If large transparent or translucent pieces are desired, the sugar must be cooked to a higher temperature (see *Cooking Process* in chapter 2).

Latex or Polyvinylchloride (PVC) gloves can be used to aerate the hot sugar. Although the gloves provide some relief from the sugar's high temperature, they usually make it more difficult to gauge the temperature of the sugar by touch.

As soon as the sugar reaches the working temperature, quickly but smoothly pull the sugar out into an even coil, then fold it back into a ball while twisting and squeezing to remove air bubbles from the hot sugar (fig. 3–5). Continue to pull rapidly, twist, and squeeze the sugar until it has cooled to the stop-aeration temperature (approximately 140°F). The sugar is still very hot at the stop-aeration temperature, and it is approximately half as soft as it is at the working temperature. Return the sugar to the rectangular building shape and repeat the building process until the sugar reaches the working temperature again. The aeration and building steps are repeated until the sugar turns fully opaque. To avoid possible crystallization, do not attempt to aerate when the temperature of the sugar drops below the stop-aeration temperature.

Using a four-bulb heating system to aerate an 8-inch disk of sugar, it will take an experienced person three or four series of the building and aeration procedures before the sugar reaches an opaque state; a beginner may require as many as ten series. I recommend that a beginner start out by aerating small quantities of hot sugar, and as the hands become accustomed to the high temperature and handling techniques, work up to larger quantities slowly.

Steady practice will teach you to recognize the temperature of the sugar by its feel and visual qualities, and make a thermometer unnecessary. The sugar at the working temperature is extremely pli-

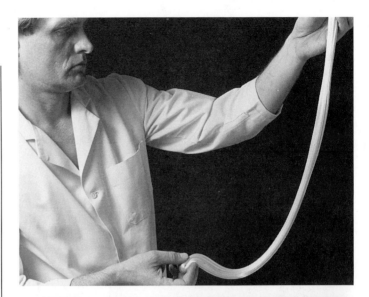

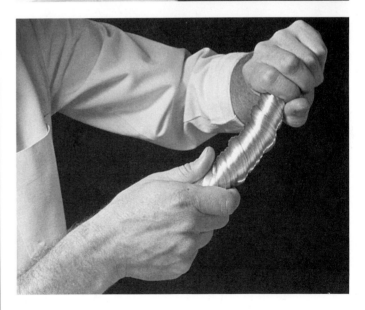

3-5. The aeration process.

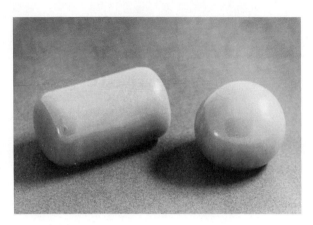

3-6. The blowing-ready cylinder and ball.

able and almost appears fluid, whereas the sugar at the stop-aeration temperature looks solid and unflexible, and is approximately half as soft.

BLOWING-READY

Blowing-ready refers to the temperature of the sugar when it is best suited for blowing (approximately 175°F). The blowing-ready temperature is the same as the working temperature.

Before blowing, all the creases must be removed from the sugar's surface. This is best accomplished by heating the creased surface for a few seconds under the infrared bulbs and then removing the creases by rubbing the sugar gently against the fabric work rack. Using a four-bulb heating system, it will take approximately 4 minutes to build an 8-inch disk of sugar into a blowing-ready shape from the stop-aeration temperature.

When the aeration is completed, return the sugar into the rectangular building shape and repeat the building process until the sugar begins to approach the blowing-ready temperature. At this point, do not lengthen the ends before folding them back to the center as in the standard building process. Instead, when a high-gloss shine covers the sugar's surface, fold the ends back to the center, and repeat this until the sugar is folded into a large mass. Before each series of folds, wait for the high-gloss shine to completely cover the sugar's surface.

Form the sugar into either a ball or a cylinder approximately two times longer than the length of the diameter (fig. 3–6). These two shapes represent the primary blowing-ready shapes. If the sugar is already at a blowing-ready temperature when aeration is completed, the final building process is not required and the sugar can be formed immediately into either blowing-ready shape.

PULLING-READY

Pulling-ready refers to the temperature range at which the sugar is best suited for pulling (100°F to 130°F).

When the aeration is completed, return the sugar

to the rectangular building shape and place it on a fabric work rack to cool. The surface of the sugar touching the work rack will cool faster than the surface exposed to the air. In order to maintain a uniform temperature, the sugar must be turned over approximately every 60 seconds.

An 8-inch disk of sugar will take approximately 4 minutes to cool from the stop-aeration temperature to a pulling-ready temperature. Test the sugar by pulling out a small thin piece (see chapter 4). If the piece is extremely supple and collapses easily, the sugar is too hot and needs to be cooled further. Conversely, if the piece cracks and breaks while you are attempting to pull it, the sugar is too cold and needs to be built up to the pulling-ready temperature. (The sugar-pulling procedures are described in detail in chapter 4.)

CRYSTALLIZATION

When tiny particles begin to appear throughout the sugar during the reheating process, it is an indication the sugar has started to crystallize. Once the sugar starts to crystallize, continued heating and handling will accelerate the process. The crystallization spreads through the sugar like a snowball rolling down a hill; one crystal produces another until the entire piece of sugar is crystallized.

Crystallization occurs when: the sugar has been improperly cooked or stored; the sugar is overheated during the reheating process; the sugar is handled at a cooler than recommended temperature, especially during the building and aerating procedures.

If crystallization starts early in the reheating process, the source of the problem is usually in the cooking or storing procedures. To find the problem, work with at least two other pieces of sugar from the same cooking batch. If they also crystallize early in the reheating process, discard the entire batch and recheck your cooking and storing procedures, as well as all your equipment and ingredients.

If crystallization occurs later in the reheating process, the sugar is either being overheated or handled when its temperature is cooler than the recommended temperature. To solve that problem, recheck

the proper procedures. Then start by using small pieces of sugar and work slowly through the reheating process until the sugar is without crystals.

If the sugar is only partially crystallized, it can be blown or pulled successfully, but all the subsequent finished pieces will display the tiny crystals throughout their surfaces. Furthermore, crystallized finished pieces will not last as long or be as sturdy as a finished piece without crystals.

RECOMMENDATIONS FOR MASS PRODUCTION

Using vegetable oil, lightly oil the bottom of a large baking sheet. Cover the sheet with pieces of precooked sugar, maintaining at least a ½-inch space between the pieces. Place the baking sheet on the door of an open oven and set the temperature at 200°F. Large industrial ovens are best suited for this procedure, but small home ovens also can be used. It takes about 30 minutes to heat the sugar to the proximity of the working temperature. The sugar can maintain this temperature for at least 2 hours. When sugar is needed for work, it requires only a short building procedure under the infrared lamps before it reaches a working temperature.

If the sugar begins to stick to the baking sheet or appears to liquify, turn the oven down approximately twenty-five degrees. If it takes longer than 30 minutes to fully heat the sugar, turn the oven up approximately twenty-five degrees. As the sugar is removed from the baking sheet for work, immediately replace it with sugar from storage.

Establishing a production line of two or more people, each performing a different aspect of the reheating process, is the most efficient way of increasing production. The reheating process, especially the building and aerating procedures, requires a deliberate technique and cannot be accelerated without crystallizing the sugar.

CHAPTER 4

INTRODUCTION TO SUGAR PULLING

Sugar pulling is a very delicate and versatile sugar-working technique that requires less expertise than sugar blowing. It will usually yield satisfactory results from the start. When the elegant satinlike shine and fragility of pulled sugar is combined in a centerpiece with blown and poured sugar, it demonstrates the grace and remarkable range capable in sugar work. This chapter will establish the preliminary pulling procedures and the techniques used to pull the elementary sugar-pulling shapes.

PREPARING THE SUGAR

Using the procedures described in chapter 3, fully aerate an 8-inch disk of precooked sugar. Color the sugar green. After the sugar has been fully aerated, turn all but one of the infrared bulbs off. Reshape the sugar into the rectangular building shape and place it on the fabric work rack away from the heat, and allow it to cool to a pulling-ready temperature. Using a four-bulb heating system, it will take approximately 15 minutes to prepare the sugar to pulling-ready.

SATINLIKE FINISH

The beautiful satinlike finish of pulled sugar is not a physical characteristic, but the result of a surface phenomenon that distorts reflected light. The phenomenon involves only the top 5 or 6 microns of the sugar's surface (1 million microns equal 1 meter).

The surface phenomenon is created when the sugar is pulled while its surface temperature is cooler than its internal temperature. As the sugar is pulled, the surface fissures into thousands of microscopic cracks and ridges. When light reflects off this surface, it creates the illusion of a satinlike finish. The maximum effect of this illusion is achieved when the sugar is aerated to a complete opacity and pulled at the coolest temperature of the pulling-ready temperature range. Sugar at this temperature is almost too stiff to manipulate.

If the satinlike surface is exposed to excessive moisture or overexposed under the infrared bulbs, the surface cracks, the ridges dissolve, and the sugar loses its satiny finish.

Note: A satinlike finish also can be achieved on blown sugar. This is accomplished by starting the blowing process with the sugar at the coolest temperature in the pulling-ready temperature range. This procedure is very difficult to accomplish, especially on complicated blown-sugar shapes. I suggest you practice the standard blowing process before attempting this procedure.

PRELIMINARY PROCEDURE

When the temperature of the sugar is within the pulling-ready range, fold the rectangle in half and pinch down the edge of the fold to form a small band of thin sugar, approximately 1½ inches across and ¾ inch wide (fig. 4–1). With the bulk of the sugar resting on the fabric work rack, hold the band with your thumbs and index fingers pressed together at the center with its tips slightly overlapping the outer edge (fig. 4–2). Pinch down while uniformly stretching the band until it reaches the desired thickness. The band gets thinner as it is stretched and can become paper thin. The thickness of the band once it is stretched will determine the thickness of the pulled sugar. In my seminars, I have found that beginners achieve their best results by starting to pull the sugar as thick as a banana skin, and after practicing the elementary pulled sugar shapes and sizes, they can work with thinner sugar.

During the pulling process, always handle the sugar by the edges. Excessive handling will quickly cool the sugar and necessitate repeated reheating, which can cause you to spend more time reheating than pulling. Be sure to maintain a uniform thickness in your pulled sugar by pulling slowly and gradually from the band. When the piece of pulled sugar is thick at the edges and thin at the center, or vice versa, the sugar has been too hot or not at a uniform temperature when pulled. If the piece of pulled sugar is thick at the top (or start) and much thinner at the bottom, the sugar has been pulled too quickly or pulled while handling just the top edge and not from the band. When the piece of pulled sugar is thin at the top and thick at the bottom, too much sugar has been pulled from the band. Regardless of the size or shape of the intended pulled-sugar piece, always pull evenly from the band until the desired width and length is reached and never pull the piece while handling just the top edge.

Note: The thin sugar band is the starting point for all pulled-sugar pieces. The sugar must be refolded and a new band stretched for each new piece of sugar pulled.

ELEMENTARY SHAPES

The following pulled-sugar pieces represent the elementary pulled-sugar shapes used in this book. Fin-

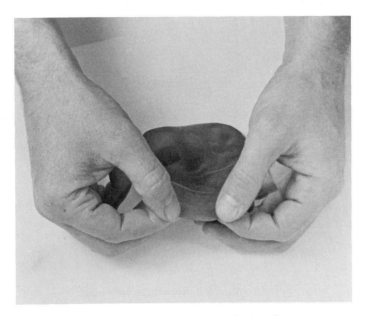

4-1. Pinch the edge of the sugar to form the band.

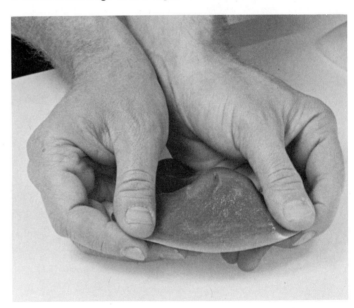

4-2. Evenly stretch the band.

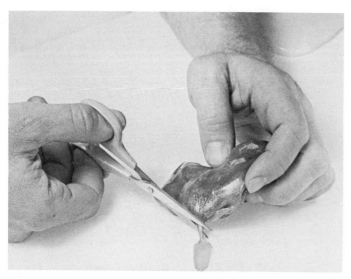

4-3. The small-sized piece of pulled sugar.

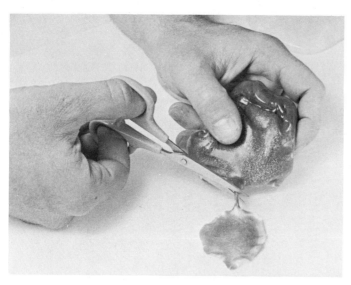

4-4. The medium-sized piece of pulled sugar.

ishing techniques, such as twisting, curling, spreading, and stretching, can be used to alter these basic shapes into the limitless pulled-sugar variations.

SMALL-SIZED PIECE: STRAWBERRY LEAF

With the nails on your thumb and index finger perpendicular to the band, carefully pinch a small point from the edge of the band. Just forward of the point, use thumb and index finger to pull an even strip, approximately ¼ inch wide and 1 inch long, from the band. Pinch the strip together at the edge of the band, creating a small thin cord (fig. 4–3); cut this cord with scissors. Keep a short length of cord at the end of the strip for the leaf stem. After folding the remainder of the cord and band into the bulk of the sugar, place it on the work rack under the infrared bulb. Hold the strip directly under the infrared bulb for approximately 5 seconds, or until the sugar is pliable, and then gently twist the strip to simulate the natural bend of a strawberry leaf (C-1). As the leaves are completed, set them on a fabric work rack away from the heat. I usually make six leaves per strawberry.

The small piece can be spread slightly wider and used for the small body feathers of a bird or the scales of a fish. When stretched and curled at the top, it also can be used for the flower petals of a carnation.

Note: Always gather the sugar into a tight mass and place it on the fabric work rack under the infrared bulb immediately after removing a piece of pulled sugar.

MEDIUM-SIZED PIECE: APPLE OR PEAR LEAF

Using the same procedure as in the strawberry leaf, carefully pinch a small point from the edge of the band. While pulling just forward of the point, use two fingers and your thumb to produce a wider strip, and slowly pull an even strip, approximately 2 inches long and 1½ inches wide (fig. 4–4). Pinch the strip together at the band, creating the leaf stem, and using scissors cut the stem. Hold the strip directly under the infrared bulb for approximately 5 seconds or until the sugar is pliable. Spread the strip carefully to create the round apple and pear leaf shape, and then gently twist the strip to simulate the natural bend of a leaf (C-1).

If the piece of pulled sugar becomes stiff or brittle while it is being pulled or altered, stop and again hold the sugar directly under the infrared bulb for a few seconds until the sugar is pliable.

The medium-sized piece of pulled sugar is the most commonly used size and can be altered into countless variations. When stretched slightly longer, it can be used as a citrus leaf (C-1). In chapter 14, it is altered to create the flower petals of the rose and tulip. A variation of the medium-sized piece is used in chapter 7 for the fins of the dolphin.

LARGE-SIZED PIECE: SWAN SIDE-FEATHERS

To maintain a uniform thickness in longer or larger pulled-sugar pieces, use one hand to pull the sugar and the other to press down on the band to maintain its thickness. Extra-wide strips of pulled sugar are created by gradually pulling up and down the length of the band until the desired width is reached.

Use four fingers and your thumb to slowly and evenly pull a strip, approximately 2 inches long and 1 inch wide, from the edge of the band. The top edge of the piece is used as the bottom of the feather and should be rounded slightly. Continue to slowly and evenly pull the strip approximately 6 inches long (fig. 4–5). Pinch the strip together at the band, forming a short, pencil-thick cord. Using scissors, cut the cord, leaving approximately ½ inch of cord at the bottom of the strip. While holding the ends of the cord, pull it into a long, thin string (fig. 4–6). Using scissors, cut the string at the end of the strip, leaving a small point. Hold the strip directly under the infrared bulb for approximately 5 seconds or until the sugar is pliable, and carefully wrinkle the strip by spreading its center wider, starting at the top and gradually working to the bottom (fig. 4–7). This technique gives the feather a natural motion (C-1).

The swan's tail-feathers use the same procedures as the side-feathers, but they are approximately half the size (C-1). When pulling the tail-feathers, use two

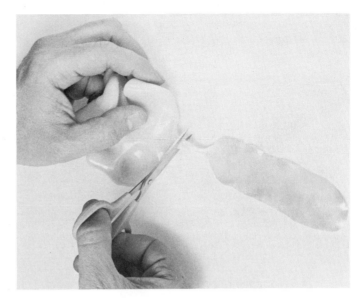

4-5. The large-sized piece of pulled sugar.

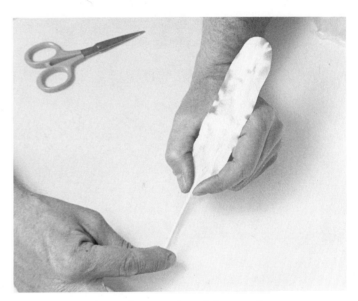

4-6. Form a point at the top edge of the swan's feather.

4-7. Carefully wrinkle the swan's feather.

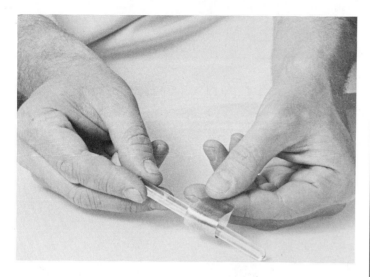

4-8. Form the ribbon loop around the large glass manipulator.

4-9. Attach the ribbon loops around the base of the cone.

4-10. Attach the bow loops directly above the bottom layer of bow loops.

fingers and your thumb to produce the narrower width.

The large-sized pulled-sugar piece is used as a tulip leaf in chapter 14. A variation of the large-sized piece is used to create the wave of water used in chapter 7. The piece also can be altered and used as the flower petals of an orchid or lily.

RIBBON LOOP

Using two fingers and your thumb, slowly pull an even strip approximately 8 inches long and 1 inch wide. Using scissors, quickly cut the strip into four 2-inch-long sections. Using a large, lightly oiled, solid-glass manipulator, bend the strips carefully around the manipulator until the ends meet to form a loop (fig. 4–8). Pinch the ends together and set the loop on its side on the fabric work rack to cool (C-2). If the strips become stiff or brittle while bending, stop and hold the strip directly under the infrared bulb until it is pliable. In chapter 12, the ribbon loops are used to decorate a candy dish.

RIBBON BOWS

A small, round ribbon bow requires 18 ribbon loops, each approximately 1 inch wide and 1 inch long, tapering to a soft point. The ends of the ribbon loops used to make the bow are pinched carefully into a soft point immediately after the ribbon loops are made (C-2).

Remove a ball of sugar approximately ¾ inch in diameter with scissors. Using your fingers, carefully form the sugar into a hollow cone, approximately 1¼ inches wide at the base, tapering to a soft point 1¼ inches high. Place the cone at the center of a small bowl, such as a ceramic custard cup. Individually heat the pointed end of the ribbon loops over the flame of an alcohol burner, and using the procedures described in the *Attaching Pulled Sugar* section of chapter 4, attach 8 ribbon loops, side by side, around the bottom edge of the cone (fig. 4–9). Using an alcohol burner, attach 5 more ribbon loops around the cone directly above the ribbon loops at the bottom (fig. 4–10). Attach the remainder of the ribbon loops around the top of the cone, remove the bow from the cup slowly, and allow it to cool by carefully holding it in front of a fan set at medium speed. When the bow is completely cooled, place it on a fabric work rack away from the heat.

Using the procedures described to pull the ribbon loop, pull an even strip approximately 1 inch wide and 12 inches long. Using scissors, remove the strip from the band and cut the strip at a 45-degree angle at the center of the strip. Carefully curl each piece and, using an alcohol burner, attach the flat ends of both pieces at the bottom of the bow angled out in a V-shape (C-2).

STRIPED RIBBON

A two-color striped ribbon is created by attaching five narrow rectangles of sugar, approximately 5 inches long, ½ inch wide, and 1 inch thick, into a rectangle 5 inches long and 2½ inches wide. Three of the narrow rectangles are the same color, and are attached at the ends and the center of the larger rectangle. The other two narrow rectangles are a different color than the first three and are attached on either side of the narrow rectangle at the center. An approximately 1½-inch-wide ribbon can be made from an approximately 5-inch long, 2½-inch wide, and 1-inch-thick striped rectangle. If a wider ribbon is desired, make the striped rectangle wider before pulling. Pinch one end of the striped rectangle carefully and evenly into a thin band, and using the same procedures as before, pull a striped ribbon.

FRUIT STEMS

Fold the sugar mass in half, and from the folded edge, pull a cylinder of sugar approximately 1½ inches long and ½ inch in diameter. Make sure the sugar cylinder is at a uniform temperature. If it is not, return the cylinder to the sugar mass, refold the sugar, and pull another cylinder. Allow the cylinder to cool on a fabric work rack until it is very firm. While holding the ends, pull the cylinder slowly and evenly into a thin cord. Using scissors, cut the cord into ½-inch pieces, and bend them slightly to simulate the stem of the fruit. Heat the top edge of the stem over the flame of an alcohol burner and, using a pin or toothpick, flare the top of the stem to create a

natural look (C-1). The apple and pear have approximately the same size stem. The orange and lemon stems are similar in size and just slightly thinner than the apple and pear. The strawberry has a very short, thin stem. For the best results, use real fruit stems or a photograph as a guide.

COIL

Using the same technique as in the fruit stem, pull two cylinders from the edge of the fold, approximately 2 inches long, and ¾ inches in diameter. When the sugar is firm, pull each cylinder slowly and evenly into uniformly thin cords. Using scissors, remove the thick sugar from the ends of the cords. Align the cords by having them touch side by side on the fabric work rack and join the pieces by pinching the ends together. While holding one end in place, slowly and evenly twist the other end until an even coil is produced (fig. 4–11). In chapter 8, the coil is used to trim and decorate the vase. In chapter 10, it is used for the Christmas ornament hooks. In chapter 11, it is used to make a base and trim the edge of a dessert cup.

ATTACHING PULLED SUGAR

Pulled-sugar pieces are welded using the flame of an alcohol burner (see chapter 1). An edge of the sugar is heated until tiny clear bubbles appear on its surface. The sugar is quickly fused in place and then very slightly pulled away from the surface to create a strong and permanent bond. Pinch the fused edge firmly to the connecting surface when welding large pulled-sugar pieces.

Note: The flame from the alcohol burner heats the sugar in three distinct stages: first, the surface of the sugar appears to liquify soon after being exposed to the flame; second, tiny clear air bubbles appear on the surface; third, tiny brown bubbles appear on the surface. To produce strong and permanent bonds, always heat the sugar to the second stage before welding and never overheat.

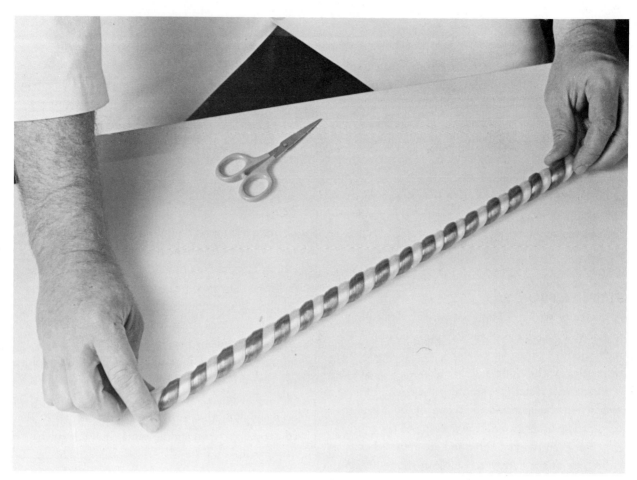

4-11. Evenly twist the cords into a coil.

RECOMMENDATIONS FOR MASS PRODUCTION

Use the mass production recommendations in chapter 3 to prepare a large mass of sugar or separate groups of different colors. The larger the mass is, the longer it will retain its temperature, which will enable you to pull several pieces before reheating is necessary.

Establishing a production line of two or more people, each performing a different aspect of the pulling process (sugar preparation, pulling, assembly), is the most efficient way of increasing production.

Note: The pulling technique requires a deliberate procedure and cannot be accelerated without negatively affecting your results.

Pulled sugar, such as stems, leaves, flowers, and ribbon bows, can be stored for 6 months or longer and still used in a centerpiece. The sugar must be stored in an airtight enclosure with Humi-sorb to achieve this longevity.

CHAPTER 5

INTRODUCTION TO SUGAR BLOWING

Although there are many easily achieved sugar-blown shapes, as well as a myriad of possible center-pieces and functional objects that can be created from these configurations, there are two fundamental sugar-blown shapes: (1) the sphere, such as an orange, apple, balloon, or Christmas ornament, and (2) the altered sphere, with its limitless variations, such as a strawberry, banana, vase, dolphin, or swan. A sphere is produced by blowing out a circular-shaped piece of blowing-ready solid sugar, whereas an altered sphere is created by blowing out a cylindrical-shaped piece.

This chapter will show the procedures used to transform basic formations into the two primary blown shapes, as well as showing all the preliminary preparations and finishing techniques required in this process.

SPHERE: ORANGE

Using the procedures described in chapter 3, fully aerate a 5-inch circular disk of precooked sugar. Color the sugar by adding a small amount of orange paste food coloring. When the sugar is fully aerated, cut it in half with scissors. Quickly flatten out both pieces into the rectangular building shape. Each piece is used to blow a large orange. Be sure to maintain a uniform thickness in each of the rectangles.

Place one of the rectangles aside in a cool corner of the fabric work rack. This piece can be used for up to 3 hours after it has been set aside, but cannot be stored and used on another day. Place the other rectangle at the center of the fabric work rack under the infrared heat. As the surface of the sugar is heated, the ends are folded back to the center, and this is repeated until the sugar is formed into a blowing-ready ball according to the procedures described in chapter 3. Using a four-bulb heating system, it will take approximately 3 minutes to build the sugar into a blowing-ready ball.

PREPARING THE BLOWPIPE

Select the appropriate blowpipe before you begin to prepare the precooked sugar. I usually use a 14-millimeter blowpipe for an orange.

As soon as the sugar has been built into a blowing-ready ball, warm the blowpipe by rotating the last $\frac{1}{2}$ inch of the pipe evenly over the flame of an alcohol burner for approximately 5 seconds, until the blowpipe is warm to the touch. Do not overheat.

ATTACHING THE BLOWPIPE

Using the large solid-glass manipulator, make a $\frac{3}{4}$-inch indentation into the top of the sugar ball (fig. 5–1). Make the indentation with a swift, even motion or the sugar will stick to the manipulator. Do not allow the manipulator to become warm before being used. Insert the warmed end of the blowpipe halfway into the indentation, leaving a small natural air

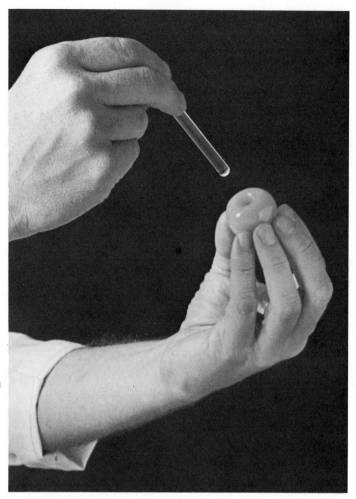

5-1. Make the indentation into the sugar with a swift, even motion.

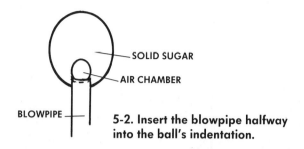

5-2. Insert the blowpipe halfway into the ball's indentation.

5-3. Hold the blowpipe slightly above parallel.

chamber in the sugar ball (fig. 5–2). When you begin to blow, the natural air chamber promotes the forward and even expansion of the air chamber. Pinch down the edges of the sugar onto the blowpipe to ensure an airtight bond between sugar and blow-pipe.

BLOWING PROCESS

As you begin to blow, hold the blowpipe and sugar ball slightly above parallel to the ground (fig. 5–3). While slowly and evenly rotating, blow softly through the blowpipe until the natural air chamber expands at the end of the blowpipe (fig. 5–4). Do

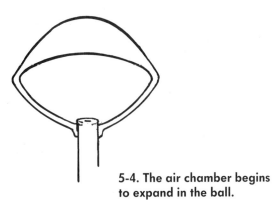

5-4. The air chamber begins to expand in the ball.

5-5. Use your fingers to restrict the outward expansion of the air chamber.

not allow the sugar to twist during the rotation. Continue rotating and blowing softly. Without squeezing, circle your fingers around the expanding surface of the air chamber to restrict its outward expansion, which allows the air chamber to move forward uniformly through the ball (fig. 5–5). As you continue to rotate and blow softly, your fingers should follow the expanding air chamber until the air chamber has penetrated the ball completely (fig. 5–6). Be sure to maintain an even thickness throughout the wall of the blown ball. This is best achieved by blowing slowly and softly. It will take approximately 2½ minutes to complete this step.

When you hold the blowpipe and sugar straight up, perpendicular to the ground during the blowing process, gravity assists in producing a squat sphere, such as a tomato, grapefruit, or candy dish. When you hold the blowpipe straight down and perpendicular to the ground during the blowing process, gravity assists in producing an oval shape, such as a lemon, pear, or wine glass. When the blowpipe and sugar are held parallel to the ground during the blowing process, you are in the best position to blow a sphere with minimal influence from gravity.

During the blowing process, stop at least once every 30 seconds to hold the sugar up for inspection. After rotating the sugar a complete 360 degrees, make certain the blowpipe extends on a straight line leveled through the center of the sugar sphere. Do not allow the sphere to angle off from the end of the blowpipe. Use your hands to make any necessary adjustments in this alignment.

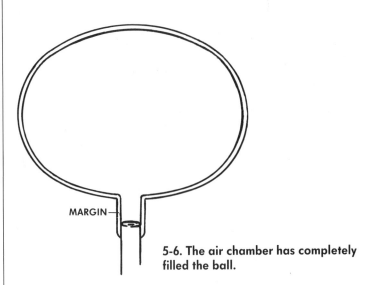

MARGIN

5-6. The air chamber has completely filled the ball.

To correct uneven wall thickness in the blown surface during the blowing process, continue to rotate and blow while using your hands to restrict the outward expansion of the thin-walled areas. This will allow the thin-walled areas to cool and not burst while the thicker-walled areas expand to create a more uniform wall thickness.

Continue to rotate the blowpipe and the sugar, while blowing slowly and steadily, until the sugar sphere has expanded to the size of an orange. A small orange is about 3 inches in diameter; a large orange is 4 inches. It should take approximately 3 minutes to complete this step.

If the sugar becomes too cold to blow before you have achieved the desired size, rotate the sphere directly under an infrared lamp until the sugar is warm enough to continue blowing. The results from reheating can be both inconsistent and unpredictable, depending on the uniformity in the sphere's wall thickness; the more uniform the wall thickness, the better your results. It is always best to avoid reheating the sugar during the blowing process.

MARGIN

Always maintain at least a ½-inch margin between the end of the blowpipe and the start of the blown sphere (fig. 5–6). This is achieved in two ways: (1) after every rotation of the blowpipe, push the blown piece away from the blowpipe by pinching down between the end of the blowpipe and the start of the blown sphere; and (2) carefully pull the sphere away from the end of the blowpipe each time you stop during the blowing process. Maintaining a margin will allow you to remove the sugar from the blowpipe without damaging any of the blown piece.

COOLING PROCESS

Cool the orange by rotating it directly in front of a fan set on high. Keep the blowpipe leveled on a straight line running through the center of the orange. Only handle the sugar when necessary to correct this alignment. Additional blowing should be done only to remove unwanted indentations such as finger marks. It can take up to four minutes to completely cool the orange.

Until the blown sugar piece is totally cooled throughout its surface, it is not completely finished. Test the temperature of the blown sugar by touching it to your lips or against the skin on the inside of your wrist. If any warmth is detected, continue to cool until all the warmth is removed.

ALTERED SPHERE: BANANA

Using the procedures described in chapter 3, fully aerate a 6-inch circular disk of precooked sugar. Color the sugar by adding a small amount of yellow paste food coloring. When the sugar is fully aerated, cut it in half with scissors. Quickly flatten out both pieces into the rectangular building shape. Each piece is used to blow a large banana. Be sure to maintain a uniform thickness in each of the rectangles. Place one of the rectangles aside in a cool corner of the fabric work rack. This piece can be used for up to 3 hours after it has been set aside, but cannot be stored and used another day. Place the other rectangle at the center of the fabric work rack under the infrared heat. As the surface of the sugar is heated, the ends are folded back to the center, and this is repeated until the sugar is formed into a blowing-ready cylinder according to the procedures described in chapter 3. Regardless of the volume of sugar, a blowing-ready cylinder is always two times longer than the length of its diameter. Using a four-bulb heating system, it will take approximately 3 minutes to build the sugar into a blowing-ready cylinder.

PREPARING THE BLOWPIPE

Select the appropriate blowpipe before you begin to reheat the precooked sugar. I usually use a 10-millimeter blowpipe for a banana.

As soon as the sugar has been built into a blowing-ready cylinder, warm the blowpipe by rotating the last ½ inch of the pipe evenly over the flame of an alcohol burner for approximately 10 seconds, until the blowpipe is warm to the touch. Do not overheat.

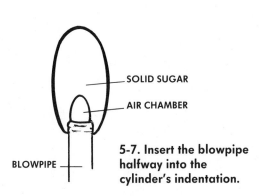

SOLID SUGAR

AIR CHAMBER

BLOWPIPE

5-7. Insert the blowpipe halfway into the cylinder's indentation.

5-8. The air chamber begins to expand in the cylinder.

ATTACHING THE BLOWPIPE

Using the large solid-glass manipulator, make a ¾-inch indentation into the center of either end of the sugar cylinder. Make the indentation with a swift, even motion or the sugar will stick to the manipulator. Do not allow the manipulator to become warm before being used. Insert the warmed end of the blowpipe halfway into the indentation, leaving a small natural air chamber in the sugar cylinder (fig. 5–7). When you begin to blow, the natural air chamber promotes the forward and uniform expansion of the air chamber. Pinch down the edges of the sugar onto the blowpipe to secure an airtight bond between sugar and blowpipe.

BLOWING PROCESS

As you begin to blow, hold the blowpipe and sugar cylinder at or slightly above parallel to the ground to prevent gravity from lengthening the cylinder. While slowly and evenly rotating, blow softly through the blowpipe until the natural air chamber expands at the end of the blowpipe (fig. 5–8). Do not allow the sugar to twist during the rotation. Without squeezing, circle your fingers around the expanding surface of the air chamber to restrict its outward expansion (fig. 5–9), which allows the air chamber to move forward uniformly through the cylinder. As you continue to rotate and blow softly, your fingers should follow the expanding air chamber until it has penetrated three-fourths of the cylinder (fig. 5–10). Do not allow the cylinder to lengthen

5-9. Use your fingers to restrict the outward expansion of the air chamber.

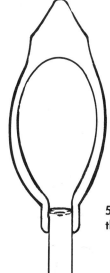

5-10. The air chamber has filled three-fourths of the cylinder.

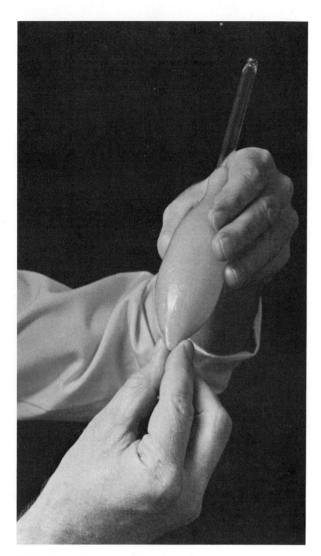

5-11. Form the banana's pointed end.

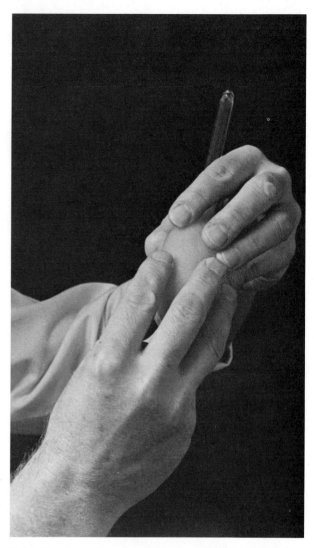

5-12. Slowly and carefully lengthen the air chamber.

until the air chamber has filled three-fourths of its length. Be sure to maintain a uniform thickness throughout the wall of the blown section. This is best achieved by blowing slowly and softly. It will take approximately 4 minutes to complete this step.

Note: Only handle the sugar cylinder by the expanding air chamber; be careful not to touch the solid sugar end. Excessive handling of the solid sugar end will cool the sugar prematurely and make it impossible to blow without reheating. Rotating only the cold section of the sugar directly under an infrared lamp is sometimes an effective method of reheating, although the results can be very inconsistent and unpredictable. For the best results, try to avoid reheating the sugar during the blowing process.

To correct uneven wall thickness in the blown surface during the blowing process, continue to rotate and blow while using your hands to restrict the outward expansion of the thin-walled areas. This will allow the thin-walled areas to cool and not burst while the thicker-walled areas expand to create a more uniform wall thickness.

While gently holding the air chamber with one hand, pinch down the very end of the solid sugar cylinder with the finger tips on the other hand to form the banana's end (fig. 5–11). Using both hands, gently grip the air chamber so that the finger tips on each hand meet at and around the center of the air chamber (fig. 5–12). By slowly and evenly pulling, extend the air chamber approximately 2 inches, then blow softly through the pipe to reshape the cylinder and remove any indentations from the sugar's surface.

With one hand at the end of the blowpipe and the other at the top of the banana, pull the sugar down from the end of the blowpipe to form the banana's stem (fig. 5–10). Be careful not to close off the air chamber. With the cylinder held down perpendicular to the ground while blowing, continue to rotate and blow, using your hands to restrict and control the outward expansion of the air chamber. Alternate equally between blowing the cylinder and pulling the air chamber, until the cylinder has reached its intended length and width (fig. 5–13). This amount of sugar can make a banana approximately 7 inches long and 1¾ inches in diameter. Do not perform the blowing and pulling procedures simultaneously; for the best results, alternate often between the two procedures. To create the bend of the banana, place the cylinder in the open palm of one hand with the end of the banana extending to the tips of your fingers. Slowly begin to cup your hand while very softly blowing to remove any creases on the surface of the sugar.

Note: Stop frequently during the blowing process to inspect the proportions of the altered sphere. Make certain the blowpipe extends on a straight line lev-

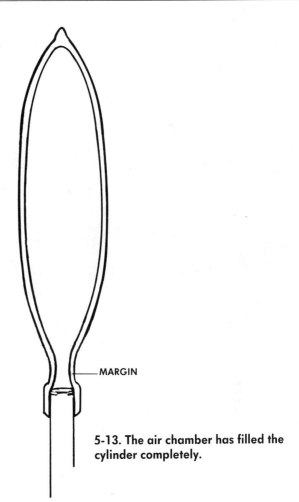

MARGIN

5-13. The air chamber has filled the cylinder completely.

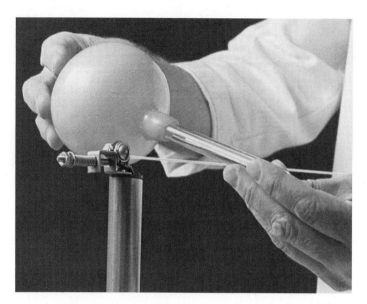

5-14. Hold the margin over the hot wire.

eled with the center of the sugar cylinder. Do not allow the sugar to angle off from the end of the blowpipe.

COOLING PROCESS

Cool the banana by rotating it directly in front of a fan set on high. Additional blowing should be done only to remove unwanted indentations, such as finger marks. After the banana has cooled, use a little brown paste food coloring to simulate ripeness in the banana. Apply the food coloring, using either your finger or a stiff-bristle brush. For the best results, use a real banana as a model.

It can take up to four minutes to cool the banana completely.

REMOVING THE BLOWPIPE USING A WIRE CUTTER

The hot-wire cutter originally was designed to split a blown-sugar sphere to create a dessert cup, a candy dish, a vessel for a wine glass, and many other functional and decorative pieces. The wire cutter also has proven to be the most efficient means for removing the blowpipe from blown sugar after the blowing process is completed.

Position the hot-wire cutter on a table top, directly in front of you, with the hot wire perpendicular to your body. Turn the cutter on by setting the automatic turn-off dial on 2 minutes. Place the piece at the far end of the hot wire, with the margin between the end of the blowpipe and the start of the blown-sugar piece, just slightly above the hot wire's surface (fig. 5–14).

While slowly pulling the sugar toward you along the length of the wire, simultaneously push the sugar down very slowly through the wire. Using scissors, quickly remove any jagged edges or unwanted sugar from the blown-sugar piece. Do not attempt to use scissors on cold sugar. If necessary, reheat the sugar over the flame of an alcohol burner. Allow the top to cool in front of a fan set on high, and then put it safely aside to await any additional finishing procedures. All of the blown-sugar pieces in this book can use this method.

After the blowpipes have been removed from the orange and banana, attach a stem and two leaves to the orange (see *Elementary Shapes* and *Attaching Pulled Sugar* in chapter 4), and place the orange and banana on a fabric work rack away from the heat (C-3).

REMOVING THE BLOWPIPE USING AN ALCOHOL BURNER

Without directly exposing the blown sugar to the flame, rotate the margin between the end of the blowpipe and the start of the blown-sugar piece evenly over the flame of an alcohol burner. Move the sugar in and out of the flame, so as not to overheat and cause the sugar to caramelize. Heat the sugar margin until the sugar becomes warm enough to bend the blowpipe easily.

Using scissors, cut through the sugar margin at the top of the blown-sugar piece and allow the top to cool in front of a fan set on high. Using a pin or the sharp point of the scissors, poke a pin-size hole in the top of the blown-sugar piece. Gases and excess air pressure build up in a blown-sugar piece when you use the alcohol flame to remove the blowpipe. If this pressure is not relieved by piercing a hole, the piece might crack, swell, or break down prematurely.

SPLITTING A SPHERE USING A WIRE CUTTER

Position the hot-wire cutter on a table top directly in front of you, with the hot wire perpendicular to your body. Turn the cutter on by setting the automatic turn-off dial on 2 minutes. Place the sphere at the center of the hot wire with the site at which the sphere is to be severed just slightly above the surface of the wire.

Simultaneously rotate the blowpipe while lightly contacting the sphere to the surface of the hot wire. Rotate the blowpipe until the sugar's surface is scored around the circumference of the sphere. Do not push down or allow the hot wire to cut through the surface of the sphere.

Place the sphere at the far end of the hot wire with the scoreline directly above the hot wire's surface. With one hand on the blowpipe and the other holding the end of the sphere, simultaneously pull the sphere toward you along the length of the wire, while gently pushing the sphere down very slowly through the wire until the sugar is completely severed (fig. 5–15).

Using scissors, quickly remove any jagged edges or unwanted sugar from the brims on both sides of the severed sphere. Remove the blowpipe from the semisphere and allow both semispheres to cool in front of a fan set on high.

Except for using a knife heated over the flame of an alcohol burner as a cutting tool, or heating the end of the sphere over the flame and using scissors to remove the top of the sphere, creating a level and smooth edge, I know of no other tool or method that can replace the hot-wire cutter in splitting a blown-sugar sphere.

RECOMMENDATIONS FOR MASS PRODUCTION

Fully aerate several pieces of precooked sugar together into either one large mass or separate groups of assorted colors. Place the sugar pieces on a fabric work rack under an infrared lamp with the dimmer switch turned down slightly (do not allow the sugar to overheat). Periodically fold the hotter surface sugar into the center of the mass. Folding the hotter surface sugar into the center develops a uniform temperature throughout the sugar and prevents crystallization, which is caused by overheating the surface sugar.

When the sugar is needed for blowing, remove the required amount with scissors, and using the building technique described in chapter 3, form the sugar into the desired preblowing shape (i.e., ball or cylinder).

Dry ice (1 pound minimum), placed a few feet behind a fan set on high speed, will deliver a cool, dry vapor through the fan, which can substantially

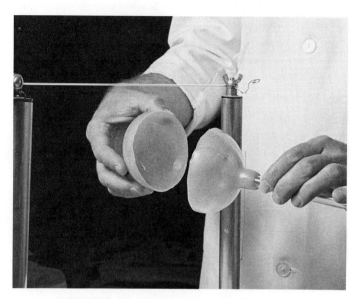

5-15. Push the sugar gently through the hot wire.

reduce the time required to cool sugar-blown objects.

Establishing a production line of two or more people, each performing a different aspect of the blowing process (preparation, blowing, and finishing) is the most efficient way of quickly producing a large quantity of finished work while also maintaining a consistency in your final results. The actual blowing process requires a slow and deliberate technique to achieve consistent satisfactory results and cannot be accelerated without negatively affecting your results.

PART 2
DECORATIVE BLOWN SUGAR

CHAPTER 6

FRUIT BOWL

Sugar-blown fruit displays can give a banquet table or a dessert cart a delightful finishing touch. Fruit provides the beginning sugar blower with a manageable project. The procedures used to create the sugar fruit are a combination of the primary sugar-blowing techniques. The sugar-pulled fruit leaves and stems also are a combination of the primary sugar-pulling techniques. Mastering the various fruit shapes will help you to develop the skills necessary to create more complicated shapes. Refer to chapter 5 for the procedures used to create the banana and the orange.

The procedures used to prepare precooked sugar for blowing and pulling are described in detail in chapter 3. I recommend that you reread the preliminary procedures before you begin your first project.

Sugar Preparation Summary: Heat the sugar disk until it is pliable. Turn the sugar over and heat the sugar until a high-gloss shine covers its surface. Add food coloring at the center of the sugar disk, then fold the disk in half and shape it into the rectangular building shape. Heat the surface of the rectangle until the high-gloss shine appears, then build the sugar by pulling the ends of the rectangle out and looping them back, with the ends meeting at the center of the rectangle. Repeat this procedure until the sugar reaches the working temperature, then begin to aerate the sugar. When the sugar cools to the stop-aeration temperature, reheat the sugar by building it back to the working temperature. Alter-

nate between reheating and aeration until the sugar is fully aerated.

GRAPE

A bunch of grapes can be formed quickly by rolling small pieces of solid sugar between your palms, creating a grape-sized ball. The balls are used as the foundation for the bunch of grapes and blown-sugar grapes are then attached over the solid-sugar balls. The smaller, light green or red table grapes use the same procedures as the larger grapes, but are approximately one-half the size.

1. Using the process described in chapter 3, fully aerate an 8-inch-diameter disk of precooked sugar. Color the sugar purple by adding equal amounts of red and blue food coloring. An 8-inch-diameter disk of sugar can be blown into approximately 35 large grapes. After the sugar is fully aerated, position the beam from one of the infrared bulbs to one side of the fabric work rack and position the other three to the other side of the fabric work rack. Place the sugar in a tight mass on the fabric work rack under the single bulb (fig. 6–1). Prevent the mass from overheating by periodically folding the hotter surface sugar into the center. This also keeps the sugar mass at a uniform temperature. Using a four-bulb

6-1. Position one of the bulbs over the sugar mass.

heating system, it will take approximately 8 minutes to fully aerate the sugar.

2. Using scissors, remove a circular piece of sugar approximately ¾ inch in diameter from the sugar mass and flatten the piece into the rectangular building shape. Heat the surface of the rectangle until a high-gloss shine completely covers its surface. Without pulling the ends of the rectangle, fold the ends back to the center. Repeat this procedure, always waiting for the high-gloss shine to completely cover the surface before folding the ends, until the temperature of the sugar reaches blowing-ready and the sugar is folded into a tight mass. Carefully form the sugar into a blowing-ready cylinder (see *Blowing-Ready* in chapter 3).

3. Attach the blowpipe to the sugar using the procedures described in chapter 5 (see *Attaching the Blowpipe*). I usually use an 8-millimeter blowpipe to make all sizes of grapes.

4. Using the procedures described in the blowing process of an altered sphere, blow softly while evenly rotating the blowpipe and sugar until the air chamber begins to expand past the end of the blowpipe. While using your fingers to restrict the outward expansion, continue to rotate and blow softly until the air chamber penetrates through to the end of the cylinder. While restricting the outward expansion of all but the last ½ inch of the cylinder, rotate and blow softly until the air chamber at the end of the cylinder has expanded into a small sphere, approximately ¾ inch in diameter (fig. 6–2). It will take approximately 3 minutes to finish blowing the grape.

5. Using the procedures described in chapter 5 (see *Cooling Process*), allow the grape and the remaining cylinder to cool in front of a fan, and remove the blowpipe from the sugar (see chapter 5, *Removing the Blowpipe Using a Wire Cutter* or *Removing the Blowpipe Using an Alcohol Burner*). When removing the blowpipe, keep approximately ½ inch of the sugar cylinder at the front of the sphere. After the blowpipe is removed, heat the remaining cylinder over the flame of an alcohol burner and form the

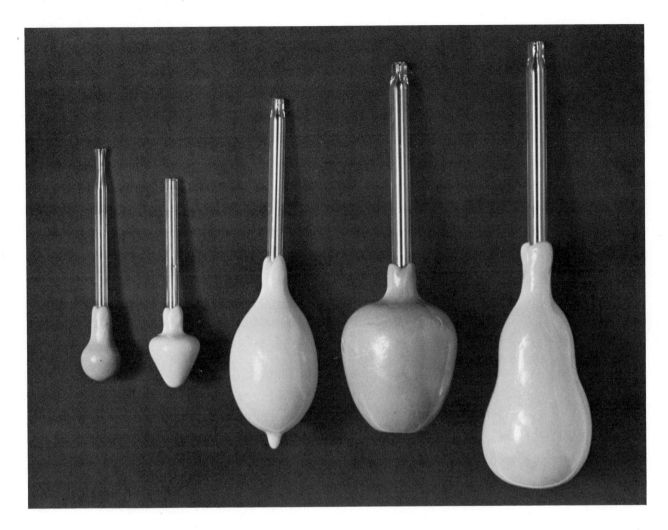

6-2. Finished blowing process of the grape, strawberry, lemon, apple, and pear.

sugar into a point. Place the grape on a fabric work rack, away from the heating system, for later assembly (C-4). Repeat the grape blowing process procedures until all of the sugar mass has been blown into large grapes.

6. The point of the sugar remaining at the front of the grapes is heated over the flame of an alcohol burner and attached to the other grapes to form a bunch. Using the procedures described to attach sugar (see *Attaching Pulled Sugar* in chapter 4), join the grapes into a bunch by attaching them one by one until all the grapes are together (fig. 6–3). For the best results, use either a natural bunch of grapes or a photograph as a model.

STRAWBERRY

The size and shape of natural strawberries varies drastically. To furnish the fruit bowl with a natural

6-3. Assemble the grapes one by one.

look, this variety must be duplicated in the sugar strawberries. The procedures here are used to blow a medium-sized strawberry, approximately 1¼ inches long, and 1¼ inches wide at the top, tapering to a rounded point at the bottom. Other sizes of strawberries also can be made using these procedures.

1. Using the process described in chapter 3, fully aerate a 6-inch-diameter disk of precooked sugar. Color the sugar by adding red and pink food coloring, using a ratio of three parts red to one part pink. A 6-inch disk of precooked sugar can be blown into approximately 12 medium-size strawberries. After the sugar is aerated, position the beam from one of the infrared bulbs to one side of the fabric work rack and position the other three to the other side of the fabric work rack. Place the sugar in a tight mass on the fabric work rack under the single bulb. Prevent the mass from overheating by periodically folding the hotter surface sugar into the center. This also keeps the sugar at a uniform temperature. Using a four-bulb heating system, it will take approximately 6½ minutes to fully aerate the sugar.

2. Using scissors, remove a circular piece of sugar approximately ½ inch in diameter from the sugar mass. Flatten the piece into the rectangular building shape and place it on the fabric work rack under the three infrared bulbs. Using the building procedures described in step two of the grape, gradually build the sugar into a blowing-ready ball.

3. Attach the blowpipe to the sugar. I usually use an 8-millimeter blowpipe to make all sizes of strawberries.

4. Using the procedures described in the blowing process of the sphere, blow softly while rotating the blowpipe and sugar evenly until the air chamber has filled two-thirds of the ball. With your fingertips, gently pull the last half of the ball into a soft point and carefully pull the ball away from the end of the blowpipe to create a margin between the end of the blowpipe and the start of

the blown piece. It will take approximately 2½ minutes to complete this step.

5. Maintain the strawberry's tapered end by using your fingers to restrict the outward expansion at the pointed end of the sphere while blowing. Continue to rotate and blow softly until the air chamber has penetrated through to the point and the strawberry has expanded to the size of a medium strawberry (fig. 6–2). It will take approximately 2 minutes to finish blowing the strawberry.

6. Using the procedures described in the cooling process, allow the strawberry to cool in front of a fan set on high.

7. To simulate the seeds from the strawberry, carefully use the point of a paring knife heated over the flame of an alcohol burner to make tiny indentations on the surface of the strawberry. Add the indentations randomly across the surface until they are distributed evenly. Stop periodically to cool the strawberry in front of a fan set on high to prevent the surface from collapsing. Using a small stiff-bristled paintbrush, add a touch of green or brown food coloring into the indentations.

8. Remove the blowpipe from the sugar and place the strawberry on a fabric work rack away from the heating system (C-4).

   Repeat the blowing-process procedures until all of the sugar mass has been blown into strawberries.

LEMON

1. Using the process described in chapter 3, fully aerate a 7-inch-diameter disk of precooked sugar. Color the sugar yellow. Using scissors, cut the sugar in half and then cut one of the halves in half. Flatten each piece into the rectangular building shape and place the large rectangle and one of the smaller rectangles on a fabric work rack away from the heating system. The large rectangle is used to blow a pear and each of the small rectangles are used to blow a lemon. Using a four-bulb heating system, it will take approximately 7 minutes to fully aerate the sugar.

2. Place the other small piece at the center of the fabric work rack under the infrared heat. Heat the sugar rectangle until a uniform gloss completely covers its surface. Lengthen the rectangle by pulling each end approximately half the length of the original rectangle and carefully fold the ends back, meeting at the center of the rectangle, as described in the building process. Always wait for the high-gloss shine to cover the sugar's surface completely before folding the sugar. As the sugar approaches the blowing-ready temperature, fold the ends back to the center without lengthening the rectangle. Continue to build the sugar until it is folded into a tight mass, then quickly form the sugar into a blowing-ready ball. Using a four-bulb heating system, it will take approximately 3½ minutes to build the sugar into a blowing-ready ball.

3. Attach the blowpipe to the sugar. I usually use a 10-millimeter blowpipe to make a lemon.

4. Using the procedures described in the blowing process of the sphere, blow softly while rotating the blowpipe and sugar evenly until the air chamber has filled three-fourths of the ball. With your fingertips, pinch the solid sugar at the end of the ball into a small point, and using the procedures described in the altered sphere, gently pull the ball into an oval shape. Quickly blow to remove any creases or fingermarks from the sugar's surface and carefully pull the oval away from the end of the blowpipe to create a margin between the end of the blowpipe and the start of the blown piece. It will take approximately 3 minutes to complete this step.

5. Using your hands to maintain the oval shape by restricting its outward expansion, continue to rotate and blow softly until the piece has reached the size of a medium lemon, approximately 3 inches long and 2 inches in diameter (fig. 6–2). It will take approximately 2 minutes to finish blowing the lemon.

6. Using the procedures described in the cooling process, allow the lemon to cool in front of a fan set on high.

7. Remove the blowpipe from the sugar and place the lemon on a fabric work rack away from the heating system (C-4). Place the other small piece at the center of the fabric work rack under the infrared bulbs and repeat the blowing process of the lemon.

Note: When the sugar is flattened into the rectangular building shape and temporarily set aside, the sugar must be reheated using the initial reheating procedures described in chapter 3.

PEAR

1. Place the piece leftover from the lemon-blowing process at the center of the fabric work rack under the infrared bulbs, and using the procedures described in step two of the lemon, build the sugar into a blowing-ready cylinder. If the sugar is cold and stiff before starting, it can take up to 7 minutes to build the sugar into a blowing-ready cylinder.

2. Attach the blowpipe to the sugar. I usually use a 13-millimeter blowpipe to make a pear.

3. Using the procedures described in the blowing process of the altered-sphere, blow softly while rotating the blowpipe and sugar evenly until the air chamber has filled three-fourths of the cylinder. Carefully pull the cylinder away from the end of the blowpipe to create a margin between the end of the blowpipe and the start of the blown piece. It will take approximately 4 minutes to complete this step.

4. While using your hands to restrict the outward expansion of the last half of the cylinder, rotate and blow softly until the front of the cylinder has expanded to a small sphere approximately 1½ inches in diameter. Carefully pull the cylinder away from the end of the blowpipe, and using your hands to restrict the outward expansion of

the first half of the cylinder, continue to rotate and blow softly until the end of the cylinder has expanded to a sphere twice as large as the front of the cylinder (fig. 6–2). Be sure to maintain a margin between the end of the blowpipe and the start of the sphere. It will take approximately 3 minutes to complete this step.

5. Using the procedures described in the cooling process, allow the pear to cool in front of a fan set on high.

6. Use an alcohol burner to remove the blowpipe from the sugar. After the blowpipe is removed, cool the top of the pear in front of a fan. After it is completely cooled, hold the pear perpendicular to the tabletop and quickly but carefully heat the top of the pear over the flame of an alcohol burner for approximately 2 seconds. Using a small solid-glass manipulator, make an ⅛-inch-deep indentation into the top of the pear, and again cool the top in front of a fan. The pear's stem is attached into the indentation.

   Using the same procedure, warm the bottom of the pear, and using the large glass manipulator, make a ¼-inch-deep indentation into the bottom of the pear. Cool the bottom in front of a fan. A small piece of green or brown sugar is attached into the indentation. After the pear is completely cooled, place it on a fabric work rack away from the heating system (C-4).

   Note: When making the indentations, never overheat the sugar. Excess heat can cause the sugar to collapse quickly. If the bottom of the pear will not be displayed, the finishing procedure is not necessary.

7. To simulate the orange, green, or brown tone often found on the surface of a pear, place small drops of paste food coloring on the surface, and using your fingertips, gently blend the color into the sugar. To simulate the brown spots on a speckled pear, dip the end of a small stiff-bristled paintbrush into a small cup of semiliquid brown food coloring. Hold the brush approximately 1 foot above the pear's surface and apply the drops

by firmly tapping the handle of the brush until the drops cover the surface evenly.

APPLE

1. Using the procedures described in chapter 3, fully aerate a 4-inch disk of precooked sugar. When the sugar is fully aerated, use the procedures described in step two of the lemon and gradually build the sugar into a blowing-ready ball. A green apple is produced by adding equal amounts of green and yellow food coloring. A red apple is produced by adding four parts red and one part black food coloring. Using a four-bulb heating system, it will take approximately 4½ minutes to prepare the sugar into a blowing-ready ball.

2. Attach the blowpipe to the sugar. I usually use a 13-millimeter blowpipe to make an apple.

3. Using the procedures described in the blowing process of the sphere, blow softly while rotating the blowpipe and sugar evenly until the air chamber has penetrated through to the end of the ball. Carefully pull the ball away from the end of the blowpipe to create a margin, and continue to rotate and blow softly until the sugar has expanded into a sphere approximately 3½ inches in diameter (fig. 6–2). To simulate the shape of a Washington State red apple, use your hands to restrict the outward expansion of the first half of the sphere after the air chamber has penetrated the ball completely and until the apple is completed (fig. 6–2). It will take approximately 6 minutes to complete this step.

4. Using the procedures described in the cooling process, allow the apple to cool in front of a fan set on high. Using the same procedure as in the pear, warm the top of the apple, and using the small solid-glass manipulator, place a small indentation into the top. Again cool the top in front of a fan, and remove the blowpipe from the sugar. If the bottom of the apple is going to be displayed, add an indentation into its bottom using the same procedure as in the pear. The

lumpy bottom of a red apple is produced by warming the bottom over an alcohol burner and using your fingers to form the lumps. After the apple is completely cool, place it on a fabric work rack away from the heating system (C-4). Additional coloring can be added using the same procedures as for the pear.

LARGE BOWL

The color for the large bowl is optional. The various techniques used to create multicolored blown sugar are described in chapter 10. Always practice on solid-colored sugar-blown pieces before attempting to use multicolored sugar. I am using light violet colored sugar for the large bowl.

1. Use the *Recommendations for Mass Production* in chapter 3 to warm three 10-inch disks of pre-cooked sugar or the equivalent. As soon as the sugar is soft, form it into the rectangular building shape and place it at the center of the fabric work rack under the infrared heat. Using the procedures described in step two of the lemon, prepare the sugar into a blowing-ready ball. Using a four-bulb heating system, it will take approximately 12 minutes to prepare the sugar into a blowing-ready ball.

2. Attach the blowpipe to the sugar. I usually use a 22-millimeter blowpipe to make the large bowl.

3. Using the procedures described in the blowing process of the sphere, blow softly while rotating the blowpipe and sugar evenly until the air chamber has penetrated through to the end of the ball and the sugar has expanded into a sphere approximately 6 inches in diameter. Maintaining a margin between the end of the blowpipe and the start of the blown ball is not required because the ball is split in half after it is completed and only the half farthest from the blowpipe is used. It will take approximately 6 minutes to complete this step.

4. Continue to rotate and blow softly until the sugar has expanded into a large sphere approximately 12

6-4. Attach the split sphere to a poured-sugar base.

6-5. Assemble the fruit bowl starting at the center.

inches in diameter. Using the procedures described in the cooling process, allow the sphere to cool completely by holding it in front of a fan set on high. The large sphere is produced using the same procedures as the small sphere. For the best results, blow slowly and steadily while rotating the blowpipe and ball evenly, and never rush the blowing process. It will take approximately 5½ minutes to complete this step.

5. Using the procedures described in chapter 5 *(Splitting the Sphere Using a Wire Cutter)*, split the sphere in half and attach the bottom half of the sphere to a poured-sugar base using the procedures described in chapter 2 *(Attaching Sugar to Bases)* (fig. 6–4).

LEAVES AND STEMS

Using the procedures described in chapter 4, pull all the fruit leaves and stems and attach them to the fruit. Pull at least 20 extra leaves for use in the fruit bowl to fill in the open spaces between fruit.

ASSEMBLING THE FRUIT BOWL

Establish a clear plan for assembling the fruit before beginning. Coil clear plastic wrap into the bowl until it is three-fourths filled, and carefully set the fruit into the bowl, starting at the center and gradually working to the edge (fig. 6–5). It is not necessary to use an alcohol burner to attach the blown sugar together or to the bowl. After the fruit bowl is assembled, the humidity bonds the fruit in place quickly and permanently. Using an alcohol burner, attach the extra leaves between the fruit and along the edge of the bowl (C-5).

CHAPTER 7

DOLPHIN

The dolphin centerpiece can add to the ambiance of an oceanside resort or supply some wishful thinking for those in snowbound or landlocked regions. Sugar-blown dolphins can be exhibited in an unlimited number of ways. This chapter will furnish a simple method for displaying the dolphins.

BLOWING PROCESS

1. Using the procedures described in chapter 3, fully aerate two 6-inch-diameter disks or the equivalent of precooked sugar. This centerpiece will use white-colored dolphins that are made by not adding any food coloring. Colored dolphins are created by adding a small drop of coloring, consisting of equal amounts of green and blue food coloring. When the sugar is fully aerated, use scissors to divide the sugar into three equal parts and individually form each piece into the rectangular building shape. One piece is used to pull the fins for the dolphin and the other two pieces are each blown into a dolphin. Using a four-bulb heating system, it will take approximately 10 minutes to fully aerate the sugar.

2. Place two of the rectangles of sugar aside on a cool corner of the fabric work rack. Place the other piece at the center of the fabric work rack under the infrared heat. Heat the sugar rectangle until a uniform gloss completely covers its surface.

Lengthen the rectangle by pulling each end approximately half the length of the original rectangle and carefully fold the ends back to the center of the rectangle as described in the building process in chapter 3. Repeat the building process, always waiting for the high-gloss shine to cover the sugar's surface completely before folding the sugar. As the sugar reaches the blowing-ready temperature, fold the ends back to the center without lengthening the rectangle. Continue to build the sugar until it is folded into a tight mass, then quickly form the sugar into a blowing-ready cylinder. Using a four-bulb heating system, it will take approximately 4 minutes to build the sugar into a blowing-ready cylinder.

3. Attach the blowpipe to the sugar. I usually use a 10-millimeter blowpipe to make a dolphin.

4. Using the procedures described in the blowing process of an altered sphere, blow softly while rotating the blowpipe and sugar evenly until the air chamber has filled three-fourths of the cylinder. Do not handle the solid sugar at the end of the cylinder while blowing, and do not allow the cylinder to lengthen before the air chamber has filled two-thirds of the cylinder. It will take approximately 3½ minutes to complete this step.

5. Pinch the edge of the solid sugar at the end of the cylinder into a point approximately ½ inch long

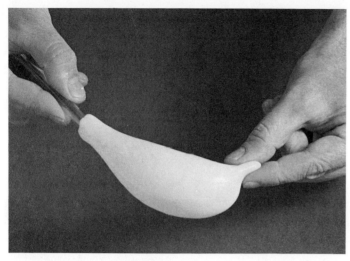

7-1. Continue to blow until the end of the cylinder is twice the size as the front.

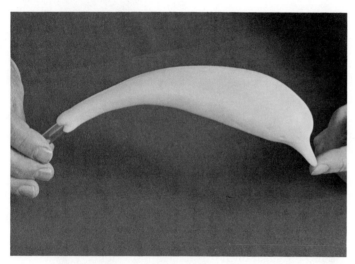

7-2. Continue to blow and lengthen the cylinder until it is approximately 9 inches long.

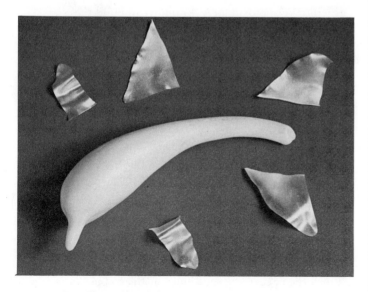

7-3. The parts of the dolphin.

and ¼ inch in diameter. Using the procedures described in the blowing process of the altered sphere, carefully lengthen the air chamber approximately 2 inches. While using your hands to restrict the outward expansion of the front half of the air chamber, continue to rotate and blow softly until the air chamber has penetrated through to the point at the end of the cylinder.

6. With one hand restricting the outward expansion of the front half of the cylinder, and the thumb and index finger on the other hand gently holding slightly in front of the point, continue to blow softly without rotating until the last half of the cylinder has expanded approximately twice the size of the front (fig. 7–1). While you are blowing, your thumb should restrict the downward expansion of the air chamber in front of and below the point. This keeps the bottom of the point level with the bottom of the air chamber. Your index finger should restrict the forward expansion of the air chamber in front of and above the point, to create an almost flat, perpendicular forehead. Carefully lengthen the first three-fourths of the cylinder approximately 3 inches. While alternating equally between blowing and pulling the first three-fourths of the cylinder, slowly curve the entire cylinder until the air chamber is approximately 9 inches long (fig. 7–2). Do not pull the air chamber while blowing. For the best results, perform the blowing and pulling procedures separately. It will take approximately 4 minutes to complete the blowing process.

7. Using the procedures described in the cooling process, allow the sugar to cool completely in front of a fan set on high. Remove the blowpipe from the sugar with an alcohol burner. Immediately after removing the blowpipe, form the soft sugar at the tail of the dolphin into a tapered point. Cool the tail in front of a fan and place the dolphin on a fabric work rack away from the heat (fig. 7–3).

Place one of the remaining sugar rectangles at the center of the fabric work rack under the heat, and build it gradually into a blowing-ready cylinder and repeat the dolphin-blowing process.

PULLED-SUGAR FINS

1. Place the remaining sugar rectangle at the center of the fabric work rack under the heat. Maintain an even temperature in the sugar while heating by turning the sugar on the fabric work rack approximately every 60 seconds until the sugar reaches the pulling-ready temperature. If the sugar is completely cooled before reheating, it will take approximately 4 minutes for the sugar to reach the pulling-ready temperature.

2. When the sugar reaches the pulling-ready temperature, turn all but one of the infrared bulbs off. Using the sugar-pulling procedures described in chapter 4, use the nails on your thumb and index finger to pull a small point from the edge of the band. While pulling just forward of the point, slowly and evenly pull the point at a 45-degree angle from the edge of the band, creating a strip resembling a right-angle triangle. The two sides of the triangle that meet at a right angle should each be approximately 1½ inches long. Using scissors, remove the triangular strip along the edge of the band. Carefully curve the bottom edge of one of the sides that meet at a right angle to conform to the curve of the dolphin's back. This piece is attached just forward of the middle of the dolphin's back to create the dorsal fin. When completed, place the piece on a fabric work rack away from the heat (fig. 7–3).

3. Using the sugar-pulling procedures, pull two more dorsal fin shapes. On one of the equal sides of each of the right-angle triangles, carefully curve the point opposite the right angle. These two pieces are attached at either side at the end of the dolphin, creating the tail. Place the pieces as they are completed on a fabric work rack away from the heat (fig. 7–3).

4. Using the sugar-pulling procedures, pull a soft point from the edge of the band. While pulling just forward of the point, pull a strip, approximately ¾ inch wide and 1½ inches long, slowly and evenly from the edge of the band. Using scissors, remove the strip along the edge of the band. Carefully curl the strip to create motion and place it on a fabric work rack away from the heat. Using the same procedures, pull another strip approximately the same size and shape, and place it on a fabric work rack away from the heat (fig. 7–3). These pieces are attached to the lower front on either side of the dolphin to create the side fins.

5. Using the sugar-pulling procedures, pull another five-piece set of dolphin fins, which are used to complete the other dolphin.

6. Individually heat the bottom edges of the dolphin fins, and using the procedures described in chapter 4, attach them to the dolphins. After the fins are attached, allow the fins to cool in place by carefully holding the dolphin in front of a fan. After it is completed, place the dolphin on top of a rolled-up towel covered with fiberglass screening (fig. 7–4).

PULLED-SUGAR WAVE

1. Using the procedures described in chapter 3, fully aerate a 12-inch disk of precooked sugar. Color the sugar by adding a small amount of blue food coloring. When the sugar is fully aerated, form the sugar into the rectangular building shape and place it on a fabric work rack away from the heat. Allow the sugar to cool to the pulling-ready temperature. Every 60 seconds turn the sugar over on the fabric work rack to maintain an even temperature in the sugar. Using a four-bulb heating system, it will take approximately 9 minutes to prepare the sugar to a pulling-ready temperature.

2. Using the sugar-pulling procedures, slowly and evenly pull a 2½-inch-wide strip from the edge of the band. Continue to pull the strip slowly and evenly while maintaining the same width until the strip is approximately 16 inches long.

7-4. Place the dolphin on a rolled towel covered with fiberglass screening.

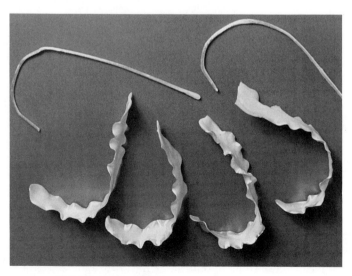

7-5. The wave strips.

Remove the strip along the edge of the band with scissors, and carefully wrinkle the strip by spreading its center wider, starting at the top and gradually working to the bottom. Wrinkle the top edge of the strip by wrinkling small spots until the entire length is wrinkled. This technique gives the wave strip a natural motion. Evenly curve the top 4 inches of the strip downward, creating a hook shape, and allow the strip to cool by placing it on its edge on a fabric work rack away from the heat.

Using the same procedures, pull at least fifteen more wave strips approximately the same size and shape. As they are completed, place them on a fabric work rack away from the heat (fig. 7–5).

3. Curve the top edge of two approximately 16½-inch-long thin metal rods, such as coat-hanger wire, creating the same hook shape produced in

the wave strips. Using the procedures described in chapter 14, evenly and individually coat each of the wires with sugar by passing them through the sugar slowly (see fig. 14–1). As they are completed, place them on a fabric work rack away from the heat (fig. 7–5).

4. Over the flame of an alcohol burner, heat the entire length of the side edge of one of the wave strips until the sugar is uniformly soft. While starting at the tops of both the strip and the wire, attach the strip to the sugar-coated wire by folding the edge of the strip over the wire. Approximately ½ inch of wire should extend from the bottom of the wave strip (fig. 7–6). Allow the strip to cool by carefully holding it in front of a fan, and after it is completely cooled, place it on its edge on a fabric work rack away from the heat. Using the same procedures, attach the other sugar-coated wire to the opposite side edge of another wave strip, and place it on its edge on a fabric work rack away from the heat. The two wave strips containing wire are used as the infrastructure to support the two dolphins.

5. Attach the two wave strips containing the wire on either side at the center of a poured-sugar base approximately 2 inches apart, with the sides of the wave strips containing the wire positioned on the inside (fig. 7–7).

   Using the flame of an alcohol burner, simultaneously heat a spot on the poured-sugar base and the end of the wire at the bottom of the wave strip, and while holding the wave strip with the curve pointed forward, attach the strip by carefully pushing the wire at a 45-degree angle into the base until it is completely inserted.

6. Using the flame of an alcohol burner, individually heat the bottom edge of the remaining wave strips and attach them to the poured-sugar base using the procedures described in chapter 4. Attach the wave strips directly in front, in back, and between the two strips containing the wire (fig. 7–8). Make sure the wave strips completely conceal the wave strips containing the wire.

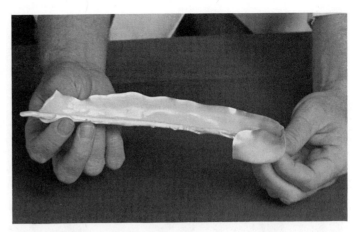

7-6. Attach the wire along the edge of a wave strip.

7-7. Attach the wave strips containing the wire at the center of a poured-sugar base.

7-8. Attach the remaining wave strips around the center of the poured-sugar base.

7. Using scissors, remove two balls of white sugar approximately ¼ inch in diameter. Individually heat the balls over the flame of an alcohol burner and attach a ball to the bottom center of each of the dolphins. Allow the ball of sugar on each dolphin to cool by holding the dolphins in front of a fan. After the sugar is cooled completely, individually heat the balls of sugar at the bottom of the dolphins and attach the dolphins onto the top of the wave strips (C-6).

CHAPTER 8

VASES

There are many sugar-blown shapes and sugar-pulled decoration techniques that can be used when creating a sugar vase. The beautiful glass-blown vases found in an abundant variety of shapes and styles can serve as excellent models for replication in sugar. This chapter will focus on the construction procedures used to create two different styles of vases: a simple bud vase and a large vase with decorative coiled handles.

BUD VASE

The color used for both vases is optional. This chapter provides the procedures used to make solid-color vases. The various techniques used to create multicolored blown sugar are described in chapter 10. Always practice on solid-colored sugar-blown pieces before attempting to use multicolored sugar. In this chapter, white sugar is used for the bud vase, and light blue and pink for the large vase.

1. Using the procedures described in chapter 3, fully aerate a 10-inch disk of precooked sugar. Add a small drop of paste food coloring to color the sugar (optional). When the sugar is fully aerated, form the sugar into the rectangular building shape and place it at the center of the fabric work rack under the infrared heat. Heat the rectangle by pulling each end approximately half the length of the original rectangle, and carefully fold the

ends back meeting at the center of the rectangle, as described in the building process. Repeat the building process, always waiting for the high-gloss shine to cover the sugar's surface completely before folding the sugar. As the sugar approaches the blowing-ready temperature, fold the ends back to the center without lengthening the rectangle. Continue to build the sugar until it is folded into a tight mass, then quickly form it into a blowing-ready cylinder.

A 10-inch disk of sugar can be blown into a small vase approximately 12 inches high, with a 4-inch-diameter base tapering to 3 inches in diameter at the top. Using a four-bulb heating system, it will take approximately 10 minutes to prepare the sugar into a blowing-ready cylinder.

2. Attach the blowpipe to the sugar. I usually use a 13-millimeter blowpipe to make a bud vase.

3. Following the procedures described in the blowing process of the altered sphere, blow softly while rotating the blowpipe and sugar evenly until the air chamber has filled two-thirds of the cylinder. Do not handle the solid sugar at the end of the cylinder while blowing, and do not allow the cylinder to lengthen before the air chamber has filled two-thirds of the cylinder. It will take approximately 4 minutes to complete this step.

4. Using the procedures described in the blowing process of the altered sphere, lengthen the air

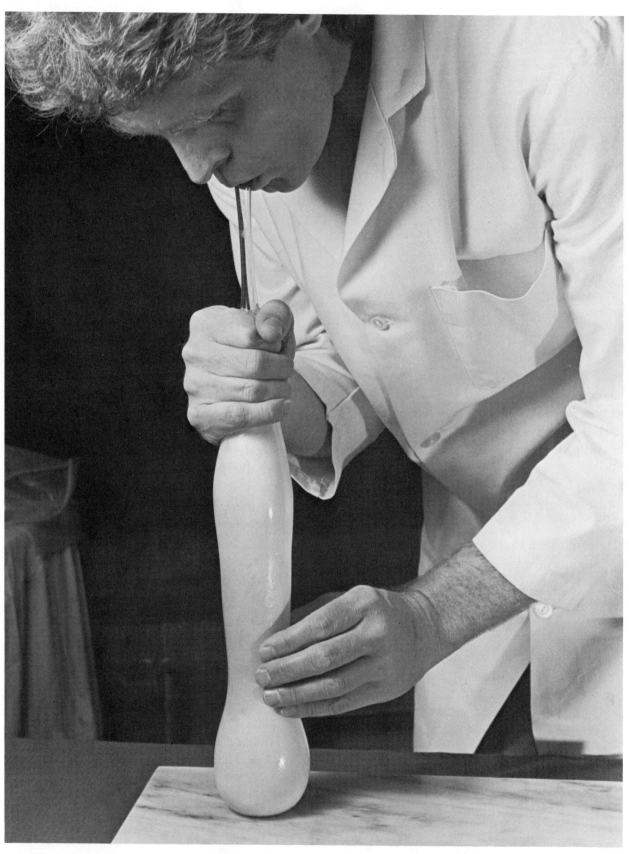

8-1. Finish the blowing process with the bottom of the sugar slightly above the surface of the marble.

chamber approximately 2 inches. Immediately after pulling, blow softly until all the creases and finger marks are removed from the blown surface.

Complete the blowing process with the blow-pipe and the sugar held perpendicular to the ground. While using your hands to restrict the outward expansion of the front two-thirds of the cylinder, continue to rotate and blow softly until the air chamber has penetrated through to the end of the cylinder. It should take approximately 2 minutes to complete this step.

5. After the air chamber has filled the cylinder, lengthen the front of the cylinder approximately 2 inches and blow quickly to remove any creases or finger marks from the surface of the sugar. With the blowpipe and sugar held perpendicular to the lightly oiled marble, and with the bottom of the sugar approximately ½ inch above the surface (fig. 8–1), rotate and blow softly while using your hands to restrict the outward expansion of all but the last one-third of the cylinder. As the end of the cylinder begins to expand, allow the bottom to touch the surface of the marble lightly on every complete rotation of the blowpipe and sugar. This will create a flat surface that will enable the vase to stand after it is completed. Continue to rotate and blow softly until the bottom of the cylinder has expanded to a sphere approximately 4 inches in diameter. Stop frequently during the blowing process to examine symmetry and wall thickness. Additional lengthening of the front of the cylinder may be necessary to maintain symmetry. It will take approximately 3 minutes to complete this step.

6. Using the procedures described in the cooling process, allow the vase to cool in front of a fan set on high.

7. Remove the blowpipe from the sugar and attach the vase to a poured-sugar base using the procedures described in chapter 4 (fig. 8–2).

Note: If the hot-wire cutter is not used to remove the blowpipe, use an alcohol burner and the alternate method described in chapter 5. After the

8-2. Attach the bud vase to a poured-sugar base.

blowpipe is removed, use the alcohol burner to heat the top perimeter of the vase, and using scissors, trim the excess sugar to create a level and smooth top.

LARGE VASE

1. Use the mass production recommendation in chapter 3 to warm three 10-inch disks of precooked sugar or the equivalent. As soon as the sugar is soft, form it into the rectangular building shape and place it at the center of the fabric work rack under the infrared heat. Add a small drop of paste food coloring (optional). Using the procedures described in chapter 3, fully aerate the sugar. When the sugar is fully aerated, form the sugar into the rectangular building shape and place it at the center of the fabric work rack under the infrared heat. Heat the rectangle until a uniform high-gloss shine covers its surface completely. Lengthen the rectangle by pulling each end approximately half the length of the original rectangle, and carefully fold the ends back, meeting at the center of the rectangle as described in the building process. Repeat the building process, always waiting for the high-gloss shine to cover the sugar's surface completely before folding the sugar. As the sugar approaches the blowing-ready temperature, fold the ends back to the center without lengthening the rectangle. Continue to build the sugar until it is folded into a tight mass, then quickly form it into a blowing-ready cylinder.

   Three 10-inch disks of sugar can be blown into a large vase approximately 20 inches high with a 7-inch-diameter sphere at the base. Using a four-bulb heating system, it will take approximately 15 minutes to prepare the sugar into a blowing-ready cylinder.

2. Attach the blowpipe to the sugar. I usually use a 22-millimeter blowpipe to make a large vase.

3. Following the procedures described in the blowing process of the altered sphere, blow softly while rotating the blowpipe and sugar evenly until the air chamber has penetrated two-thirds of the cylinder. Do not handle the solid sugar at the end of the cylinder while blowing, and do not allow the cylinder to lengthen before the air chamber has filled two-thirds of the cylinder. It will take approximately 5 minutes to complete this step.

4. Using the procedures described in the blowing process of the altered sphere, carefully lengthen the air chamber approximately 2 inches. Immediately after pulling, blow softly until all the creases and finger marks are removed from the blown surface. With one hand holding the bottom of the air chamber, and the other holding just below the end of the blowpipe, rotate and blow softly until the front of the cylinder has expanded into a sphere approximately 3 inches in diameter (fig. 8–3). Rotate the sugar quickly for approximately 30 seconds directly in front of a fan set on high. This partially cools the sphere and assists in restricting its outward expansion while the blowing process continues. It will take approximately 3 minutes to complete this step.

5. Using your hands to restrict the outward expansion of the front of the cylinder, rotate and blow softly until the air chamber has penetrated through to the bottom of the cylinder. Carefully lengthen the bottom half of the sphere at the top of the cylinder approximately 2 inches, and quickly blow to remove any creases from the blown surface.

   Complete the blowing process with the blowpipe and sugar held perpendicular to a lightly oiled marble, and with the bottom of the sugar approximately ½ inch above the surface. Continue to alternate equally between lengthening the front of the cylinder 2 inches at a time, and rotating and blowing softly while using your hands to restrict the outward expansion of the front of the cylinder, until the vase is approximately 20 inches long and the sphere at the bottom is 7 inches in diameter (fig. 8–4). Allow the bottom of the cylinder to touch the surface of the marble lightly on every complete rotation of the

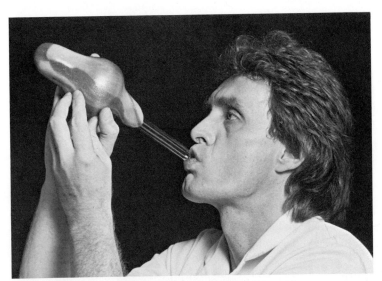

8-3. Blow the top of the cylinder into a 3-inch-diameter sphere.

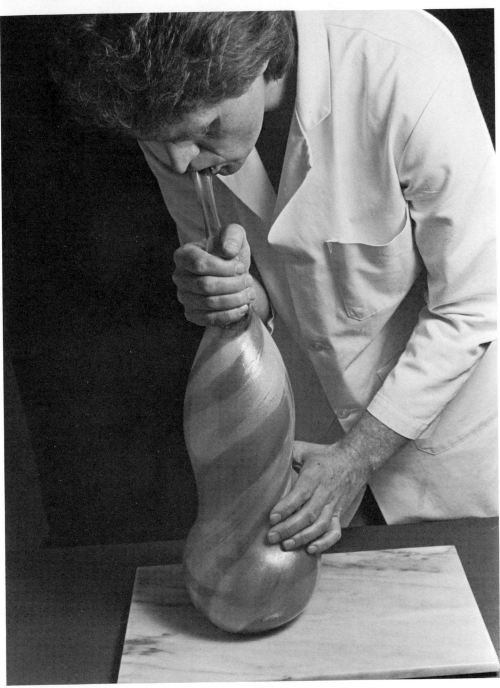

8-4. Restrict the outward expansion at the top of the vase until the bottom has expanded fully.

8-5. Curve the coils into S-shapes.

blowpipe and sugar. This will create a flat surface that will enable the vase to stand after it is completed. Stop frequently during the blowing process to examine symmetry and wall thickness. It will take approximately 5 minutes to complete this step.

6. Using the procedures described in the cooling process, allow the vase to cool in front of a fan set on high.

7. Remove the blowpipe from the sugar and attach the vase to a poured-sugar base.

Note: If the hot-wire cutter is not used to remove the blowpipe, use an alcohol burner. After the blowpipe is removed, use the alcohol burner to heat the top perimeter of the vase, and using scissors, trim the excess sugar to create a level and smooth top.

FINISHING PROCEDURES

1. Measure the top edge of the large vase with a string. Using the procedure described to create a coil (see chapter 4), form two different colored solid-sugar cylinders, each approximately 3 inches long and 1½ inches in diameter. Twist the cylinders into a uniformly thick coil approximately 24 inches long and ¾ inch in diameter, and using scissors, cut the coil into three equal pieces. Pull one of the pieces into a uniformly thick coil approximately ¼ inch in diameter, and remove a length of coil with scissors the same length as the string used to measure the top edge of the large vase. Pull both of the remaining pieces from the original coil into a uniformly thick coil the same length as the height of the large vase, and allow them to cool by placing them carefully on a lightly oiled marble. Turn the coils every 60 seconds while they are cooling to maintain an even temperature and a uniform shape. These two pieces are used to make handles for the vase.

2. Place the thin coil at the center of the fabric work rack under the heat of one infrared bulb. When the sugar is soft, circle the coil and press the ends of the coil together smoothly. While the sugar is

still soft yet firm enough to handle, carefully set the coil on the top edge of the large vase, and very slightly push the cords down onto the edge. To ensure a strong bond, heat the end of a pencil-thick stick of sugar, and tack the bottom inside edge of the coils to the inside of the vase every 90 degrees along the top circumference of the vase. Heat the coil on the edge of the large vase over the flame of an alcohol burner, and use your finger to carefully and evenly ruffle the coil along the top edge.

The best method for executing the ruffling procedure is to envision the top edge of the vase as a clock face. Make the first ruffle at the twelve o'clock position, the second ruffle at the six o'clock position, and stop to cool the edge in front of a fan. After the edge is cooled, make the next ruffle at the three o'clock position, then across at the nine o'clock position, and again allow the edge to cool in front of a fan. Continue the procedure until the edge is completely ruffled.

3. Position one of the infrared bulbs over the two lengths of coil on the marble. When the sugar is soft, turn off the infrared bulb and curve each coil carefully into identical S-shapes. Carefully invert one of the S-shapes (fig. 8–5) and allow the sugar to cool completely.

4. After the sugar is cooled completely, touch the handles to the sides of the vase while they are cold to determine their exact placement. Heat the top and the bottom end of each handle, one handle at a time, over the flame of an alcohol burner and attach the handles to the vase (see *Attaching Pulled Sugar* in chapter 4). Bond the handles to opposite sides of the large vase (C-7).

CHAPTER 9

SWAN

The swan is one of the most graceful and mystical birds in nature. Throughout history, its beauty has furnished art and literature with an aesthetic ideal. A sugar-blown swan can add a sublime finishing touch to an elegant banquet table, or when prepared on a smaller scale and filled with a dessert such as a mousse or custard, it serves as an exquisite dessert cup that makes a stunning tableside presentation.

BLOWING PROCESS

1. Using the procedures described in chapter 3, fully aerate a 10-inch disk of precooked sugar. The swan's white color is achieved by aerating to opacity. No food coloring is necessary. When the sugar is fully aerated, form the sugar into the rectangular building shape and place it under the infrared heat. Heat the rectangle until a high-gloss shine covers its surface completely. Lengthen the rectangle by pulling each end approximately half the length of the original rectangle, and carefully fold the ends back meeting at the center of the rectangle, as described in the building process. Repeat the building process, always waiting for the high-gloss shine to cover the sugar's surface completely before folding the sugar. As the sugar approaches the blowing-ready temperature, fold the ends back to the center without lengthening the rectangle. Con-

tinue to build the sugar until it is folded into a tight mass, then quickly form it into a blowing-ready cylinder.

A 10-inch disk of sugar can be blown into a swan with an oval body approximately 14 inches long and 6½ inches in diameter, and the neck approximately 16 inches long and 14 inches high when curved. Using a four-bulb heating system, it will take approximately 10 minutes to prepare the sugar into the blowing-ready cylindrical shape.

2. Attach the blowpipe to the sugar. I usually use a 13-millimeter blowpipe to make a medium-sized swan.

3. Using the procedures described in the blowing process of the altered sphere, blow softly while rotating the blowpipe and sugar evenly until the air chamber has filled two-thirds of the cylinder. Do not handle the solid sugar at the end of the cylinder while blowing, and do not allow the cylinder to lengthen before the air chamber has filled two-thirds of the cylinder. It will take approximately 4 minutes to complete this step.

4. With your fingertips, gently form the solid sugar at the end of the cylinder into a soft point and bend it upward perpendicular to the blown section (fig. 9–1). Do not squeeze or excessively handle the solid sugar end.

5. Using the procedures described in the blowing process of the altered sphere, carefully pull the air chamber into an oval shape (fig. 9–2). Immediately after pulling, blow softly until all the creases and finger marks are removed from the blown surface.

6. Finish the blowing process with the swan at the center of a fabric work rack away from the heat, placed directly in front of a fan set on medium. With one hand holding the blowpipe, and the other holding the tip of the solid sugar while blowing, continue to alternate equally between blowing and pulling the air chamber until the body is approximately 13 inches long and 6 inches in diameter. It will take approximately 3½ minutes to complete this step.

7. With one hand lightly holding the base of the solid sugar, and the other holding at the top, blow softly while slowly and evenly pulling the neck up perpendicular and proportionate to the blown body, and carefully bend it into the swan's familiar curve (fig. 9–3). I try to keep the length of the swan's neck, after it is curved, the same length as the swan's body. Additional blowing should be done only to remove unwanted indentations, such as finger marks.

8. Using the procedure described in the cooling process, allow the swan to cool in front of a fan set on high. It can take up to 7 minutes to cool the swan completely.

9. Slowly heat the last inch of the swan's neck over the flame of an alcohol burner. To prevent overheating, move the sugar in and out of the flame until the sugar is soft enough to mold with your fingers. Quickly form the head and the beak, using scissors to remove any excess sugar. Cool the head in front of a fan and remove the blowpipe from the sugar.

10. Immediately after removing the blowpipe, attach the bottom of the swan to a poured-sugar base, using the procedure described in *Attaching Sugar to Bases* in chapter 2.

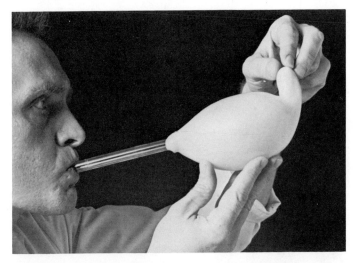

9-1. Bend the solid sugar point upward perpendicular to the blown section.

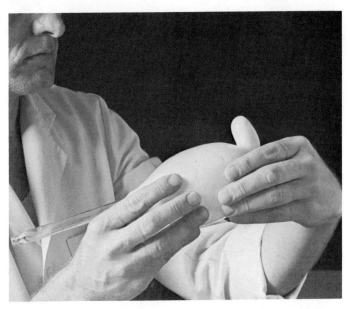

9-2. Pull the air chamber into an oval.

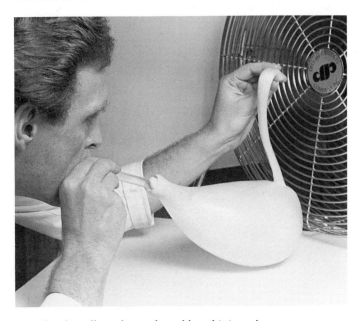

9-3. Slowly pull up the neck and bend it into the swan's familiar curve.

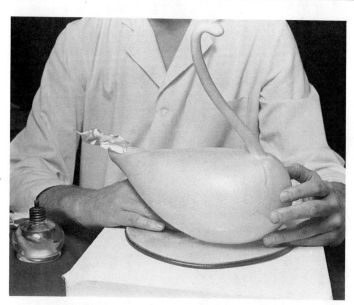

9-4. Attach a tail feather at the top of the swan's rear, slightly off center.

PULLED-SUGAR FEATHERS AND ASSEMBLY

1. Using the procedures described in chapter 3, fully aerate a 10-inch disk of precooked sugar. Do not add any food coloring. When the sugar is fully aerated, form the sugar into the rectangular building shape and place it on a fabric work rack away from the heat. Allow the sugar to cool uniformly to a pulling-ready temperature by turning it over on the fabric work rack approximately every 60 seconds. This sugar is used to pull the swan's side and tail feathers. Using a four-bulb heating system, it will take approximately 15 minutes to prepare the sugar to the pulling-ready state.

2. Using the sugar-pulling procedures used to make a swan feather, pull out a minimum of twenty-four side feathers, each approximately 8 inches long and 2½ inches wide (C-1). I sometimes use up to sixty feathers for a special food show display. Place the feathers as they are completed on a fabric work rack away from the heat.

3. Using the sugar-pulling technique, pull out six tail feathers, approximately 4 inches long and 1½ inches wide (C-1). Place the tail feathers with the side feathers as they are completed.

4. Heat the bottom edge of one of the tail feathers over the flame of an alcohol burner. Do not overheat. Attach the feather to the top of the swan's rear, slightly off center (fig. 9–4).

   Attach another tail feather to the top of the swan's rear, slightly off to the other side of the center. Another tail feather is attached to the top of the swan's rear, overlapping the edges of the first two feathers. Add the other three tail feathers to the bottom of the swan's rear, using the same procedure as the top. The tail feathers should completely encircle and conceal the swan's rear.

Note: Start the bond with the feather perpendicular to the body. Gently push down and forward until the feather conceals the bond, then lightly

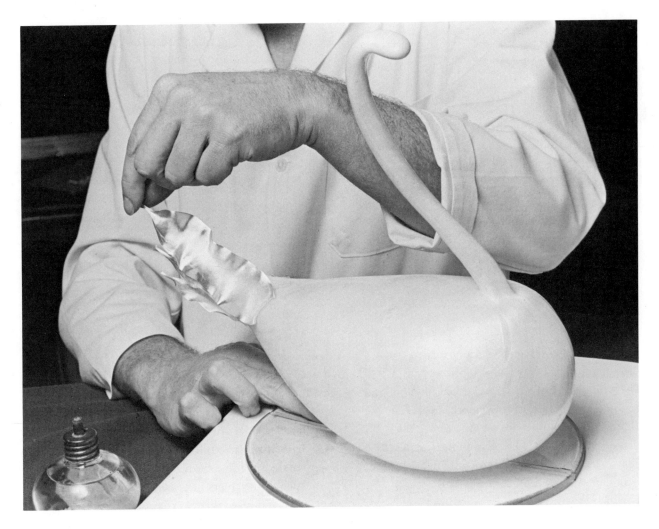

push the feather against the body. Press the hot sugar at the bottom edge of the feather firmly to the body to assure a strong and permanent bond. All the tail and side feathers are attached using this technique.

5. Heat the bottom edge of the side feathers over the flame of an alcohol burner and attach them to the body, starting at the top of the swan's rear (fig. 9–5). Attach each new feather slightly forward of the last until you reach the front of the swan. To maintain symmetry, assemble both sides simultaneously, one feather at a time. When completed, allow the feathers to cool by placing the swan headfirst in front of a fan set at low speed.

6. Using a paintbrush, apply a little black and yellow food coloring to create the swan's eye and beak. This finishing procedure is optional. Aesthetically, I feel this procedure is superfluous and often diminishes the sugar's unique beauty (C-8).

9-5. Attach a side feather at the top, on the side of the swan's rear.

CHAPTER 10

CHRISTMAS ORNAMENTS

Blown-sugar Christmas ornaments can be made as elegant and durable as ornaments of blown-crystal glass. The wide variety of shapes and decorating techniques used to create glass-blown ornaments can be duplicated easily in sugar-blown ornaments. The sugar-blown ornaments may be eaten at the end of the holidays or they can be stored carefully in an airtight container with Humi-sorb and used another year. This chapter will provide the procedures used to blow three different Christmas ornament styles, each using a different coloring technique to create multicolored blown sugar.

The ornament styles in this chapter were chosen to illustrate some of the primary procedures used in this process. These standard shapes, as well as the finishing and coloring techniques used, will provide an excellent foundation for creating more elaborate and innovative ornaments.

PREPARING THE SUGAR

1. Place four 5-inch disks of precooked sugar on the fabric work rack under the infrared heat. Do not allow the disks to touch. Using the procedures described in chapter 3, color each disk of sugar with a different color of food coloring, and separately but simultaneously aerate the sugar disks. Opaque light blue, opaque yellow, translucent pink, and transparent apple-green are used in this chapter. Alternate between reheating and aerating

the pieces until all four disks of sugar are fully aerated. To provide an added contrast to the sugar ornaments, I partially aerate two of the disks of sugar, leaving the sugar transparent in one and translucent in the other while aerating the other two disks of sugar to full opacity.

After the sugar has been aerated, individually form each of the colors into the rectangular building shape and place them at the back of the fabric work rack. Do not allow the sugars to touch. Position one of the infrared bulbs over the sugar to maintain the temperature (fig. 10–1). Using a four-bulb heating system, it will take approximately 8 minutes to aerate the four 5-inch disks of precooked sugar.

SPHERICAL ORNAMENT

1. Using scissors, remove the ½-inch strip from the end of each sugar rectangle. Place the strips at the center of the fabric work rack under the three remaining infrared bulbs. Join the strips into one piece by pressing them together carefully along their side edges and form the striped piece into the rectangular building shape (C-9). Be sure to maintain both an even stripe and a uniform thickness in the rectangle.

2. Heat the sugar rectangle until a uniform gloss covers its surface completely. Lengthen the rec-

tangle by pulling each end approximately half the length of the original rectangle, and carefully fold the ends back meeting at the center of the rectangle, as described in the building process. Repeat the building process, always waiting for the high-gloss shine to cover the sugar's surface completely before folding the sugar. As the sugar approaches the blowing-ready temperature, fold the ends back to the center without lengthening the rectangle. Continue to build the sugar until it is folded into a tight mass, then quickly form the sugar into a blowing-ready ball. Using a four-bulb heating system, it should take approximately 4 minutes to complete this step.

3. Attach the blowpipe to the sugar. I usually use a 13-millimeter blowpipe to make the spherical ornament.

4. Following the procedures described in the blowing process of the sphere, blow softly while evenly rotating the blowpipe and sugar until the air chamber has filled the ball and it has expanded into a small sphere approximately 2 inches in diameter. Pull the sphere away from the end of the blowpipe carefully to create a margin between the end of the blowpipe and the start of the sphere. Continue to rotate and blow softly until the sphere has expanded to approximately a 3½-inch-diameter sphere. Be sure to maintain the margin between the blowpipe and the sphere. It will take approximately 4 minutes to complete this step.

5. Using the procedures described in the cooling process, allow the sphere to cool in front of a fan set on high.

6. Remove the blowpipe from the sugar and place the sphere on a fabric work rack away from the heat.

SPIKED ORNAMENT

1. Using scissors, remove three 1-inch strips from the end of the sugar rectangles. I use opaque light blue, opaque yellow, and translucent pink to

10-1. Position one of the bulbs over the four sugar rectangles.

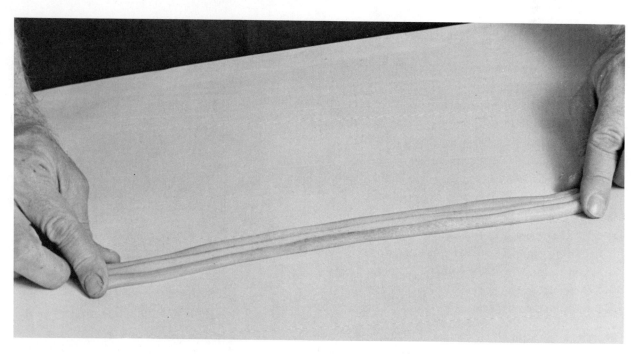

10-2. Place the cords together with their sides touching.

make the spiked ornament. Pull the strips into uniformly thick 10-inch cords and place them with their sides touching at the center of the fabric work rack under the infrared heat (fig. 10–2). When the sugar cords are soft and at a uniform temperature, pinch the ends of the cords together and twist the sugar into an even coil.

2. Wind the coil into a flat circle approximately 2½ inches in diameter and place it at the center of the fabric work rack under the infrared heat (C-9). Turn the sugar over approximately every 60 seconds to maintain an even temperature in the sugar while heating. As the sugar softens, use your fingers to periodically press the perimeter of the circle into a compact mass at the center of the fabric work rack.

3. Heat the sugar until it reaches the blowing-ready temperature and form it into a blowing-ready ball. Attach the blowpipe to the sugar. I usually use a 13-millimeter blowpipe to make the spiked ornament. Using a four-bulb heating system, it should take approximately 5 minutes for the sugar to reach blowing-ready.

4. Using the procedures described in the blowing process of the sphere, blow softly while rotating the blowpipe and sugar evenly until the air chamber has filled the ball and it has expanded into a small sphere approximately 2 inches in diameter.

Carefully pull the sphere away from the end of the blowpipe to create a margin between the end of the blowpipe and the start of the sphere. Finish the blowing process, holding the blowpipe and sugar upward, perpendicular to the ground. Continue to rotate and blow softly until the sugar has expanded into a squat sphere approximately 3½ inches in diameter (fig. 10–3). Be sure to maintain a margin between the blowpipe and sphere. It should take approximately 4 minutes to complete this step.

5. Using the procedures described in the cooling process, cool the sugar in front of a fan set on high.

6. Rotate the margin between the blowpipe and sphere over the flame of an alcohol burner. Move the sugar in and out of the flame to avoid caramelizing (browning) the sugar. When the sugar margin is uniformly soft, similar to the texture of modeling clay, slowly and carefully pull the blowpipe away from the sphere, creating a tapered spike approximately 3½ inches long (fig. 10–4). Heat the end of the spike, and using scissors, remove the blowpipe and form the sugar at the end of the spike into a point.

7. Cool the spike in front of a fan set on high and place the ornament on a fabric work rack away from the heat.

SPLIT ORNAMENT

1. Using scissors, remove one-half of the remaining transparent apple-green colored sugar, and one-half of the remaining opaque light-blue and opaque yellow colored sugar. The volumes of the light-blue and yellow colored sugar should be equal, and together they should be equal to the volume of the apple-green colored sugar. Form the apple-green colored sugar into the rectangular building shape and place it at the center of the fabric work rack under the infrared heat. Separately form the light-blue and yellow colored sugar into strips the same length but one-half the

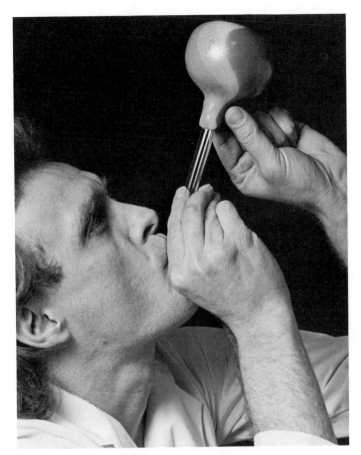

10-3. Blow the sugar into a squat sphere.

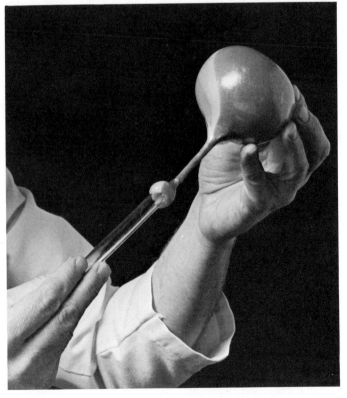

10-4. Slowly pull the blowpipe from the front of the squat sphere.

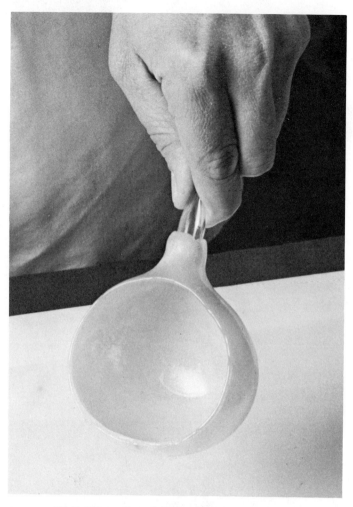

10-5. Vertically split the sphere in half without cutting the margin.

width of the apple-green colored rectangle. Place the strips on top of the rectangle completely covering its surface (C-9, at left).

2. Heat the surface of the sugar until the high-gloss shine covers its surface completely. Turn the sugar over at the center of the fabric work rack, and when the high-gloss shine covers its surface, carefully fold the ends of the rectangle back to the center. The opaque colored sugar should be at the center of the sugar mass, completely covered by the transparent apple-green colored sugar.

3. Turn the sugar over every 60 seconds to maintain an even temperature in the sugar. Use your fingers to periodically press the edges of the sugar into a compact mass at the center of the fabric work rack.

4. When the sugar reaches the blowing-ready temperature, form it into a blowing-ready ball and attach the blowpipe to the sugar. I usually use a 13-millimeter blowpipe to make the split ornament. Using a four-bulb heating system, it should take approximately 5 minutes to form the sugar into a blowing-ready ball.

5. Using the procedures described in the blowing process of the sphere, blow softly while rotating the blowpipe and sugar evenly until the air chamber has filled the ball and it has expanded into a small sphere approximately 2 inches in diameter. Carefully pull the sphere away from the end of the blowpipe to create a margin between the end of the blowpipe and the start of the sphere. Continue to rotate and blow softly until the sugar has expanded into a sphere approximately 3½ inches in diameter. It should take approximately 4 minutes to complete this step.

6. Using the procedures described in the cooling process, cool the sugar in front of a fan set on high.

7. Remove the blowpipe from the sugar. Using the procedures described to split a blown-sugar sphere, vertically split the sphere in half without cutting the margin at the top of the sphere (fig.

10–5). Cool the split sphere in front of a fan set on high.

8. Using the flame of an alcohol burner, heat a spot at the edge of the split sphere for a couple of seconds (do not overheat). When the sugar is soft, carefully use your finger to press the edge outward to create a ruffle (fig. 10–6). The best method for executing this technique is to envision the edge of the split sphere as a clock face. Make the first ruffle at the twelve o'clock position, then make the second ruffle at the six o'clock position, and stop to cool the edge in front of a fan. After the edge has cooled, make the next ruffle at the three o'clock position, then across at the nine o'clock position, and again allow the edge to cool in front of a fan. Continue the procedure until the edge is ruffled completely (fig. 10–7).

The split-sphere ornament can be filled with a wide variety of decorations, such as a sugar-pulled flower, ribbon bow, or miniature Christmas tree. I am using two small sugar coils shaped like candy canes and a small sugar ribbon to decorate the split sphere. The procedures used to make the coil and ribbon are described in chapter 4.

10-6. Use your finger to form the ruffle.

10-7. Evenly ruffle the entire edge.

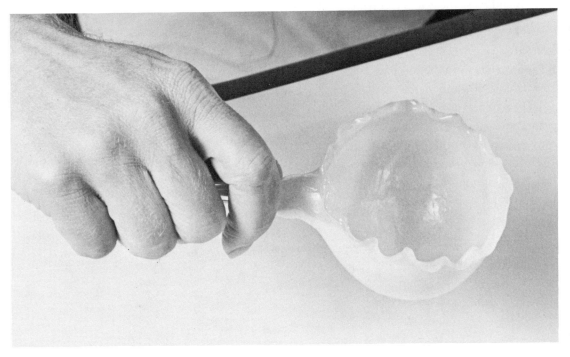

SUGAR HOOKS

The sugar hooks are made from either solid-color or multicolored sugar coil and add a beautiful finishing touch to the sugar-blown ornaments. The sugar hooks are very sturdy and can easily support the weight of the sugar-blown ornaments for up to several months. In New York City, where very high temperatures are often accompanied by high relative humidity in the summer, I hung sugar ornaments on strings anchored to the ceiling for up to 8 months. The ornaments were removed because they had collected a thick coating of dirt and dust, not because the ornaments or hooks had collapsed. I usually use the same colors in the sugar hook that were used in the sugar ornament, but many different combinations of colors can be used.

SOLID-COLOR HOOK

1. Using scissors, remove a ball of solid-colored sugar approximately ¾ inch in diameter. This size piece of sugar will make two sugar hooks. Slowly pull the sugar ball into a uniformly thick cord approximately 8 inches long. Using scissors, cut the cord in half, and place the cords together side by side on the fabric work rack. Pinch the ends of the cords and twist them into an even coil approximately 8 inches long.

2. Using scissors, remove a 3-inch length of coil, and starting at one end, wind the coil into a flat circle approximately ¾ inch in diameter. Place it away from the heat on top of the wood frame at the edge of the fabric work rack until it is cool (C-10). Using scissors, remove a 1¼-inch length of coil, form it into a hook, and place it away from the heat on top of the wood frame at the edge of the fabric work rack until it is cool (C-10).

3. When both pieces of sugar are cooled completely, heat the bottom of the sugar hook over the flame

of an alcohol burner, and attach the hook at the center of and perpendicular to the circled coil. Firmly press the warm sugar from the hook onto the circled coil to ensure a firm and permanent bond, and place it away from the heat on the wooden frame at the edge of the fabric work rack until it is cool (C-10).

MULTICOLORED HOOK

1. Using scissors, remove a ball of sugar approximately ¾ inch in diameter from each of four masses of colored sugar. Slowly pull each of the balls into identical, uniformly thick cords, approximately 8 inches long. Separately place the cords in pairs touching side by side, and place one of the pairs directly on top of the other pair. Using the procedure described to make a sugar coil, pinch the ends of the cords, and twist the cords into an even coil.

2. Make the circular-coiled base and the hook and attach the hook to the circled-coil using the procedures described in steps one and two of the solid-colored hooks. As they are completed, place the circled coil and hook away from the heat on top of the wooden frame at the edge of the fabric work rack until they are cooled (C-10).

ATTACHING THE HOOK

1. Only heat the bottom of the circled coil over the flame of an alcohol burner (fig. 10–8) and attach the hook to the margin at the top of the sugar-blown ornament.

2. Press the warm sugar from the edges of the circled coil onto the top of the ornament to ensure a firm and permanent bond (fig. 10–9). Allow the hook to cool in place by carefully holding the ornament in front of a fan. Using the same colored sugar as in the ornament, make the hooks for the other two ornaments and attach them (C-11).

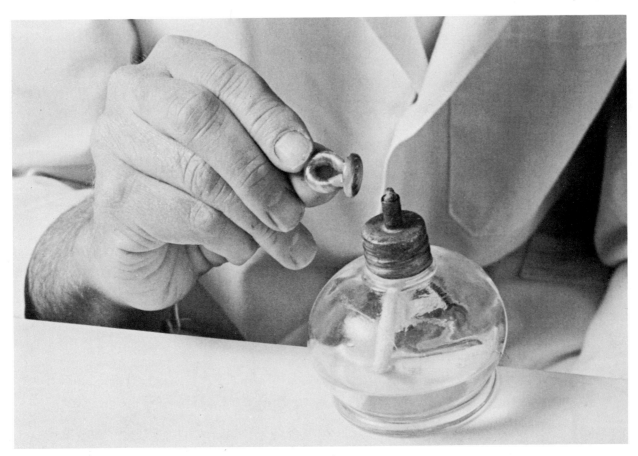

10-8. Heat the bottom of the hook over the alcohol burner.

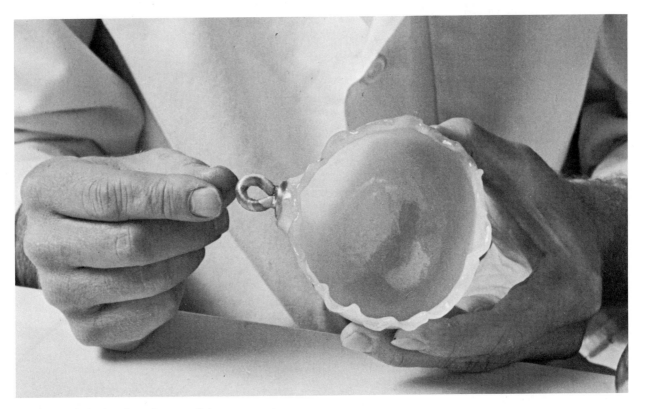

10-9. Attach the hook to the top of the ornament.

PART 3

FUNCTIONAL BLOWN SUGAR

CHAPTER 11

DESSERT CUPS

Sugar-blown dessert cups add an elegant flair to a fine meal. The dessert cups can be flavored and colored to accent their ingredients and can hold a wide variety of desserts, including mousse, custard, sorbet, ice cream, and fresh fruit. The dessert cups can be stored empty in an airtight container with Humisorb and used for up to a year. The dessert cups cannot be stored in a refrigerator or freezer. For the best results, fill the dessert cups just before serving. Desserts like sorbet, ice cream, and fresh fruit can be added up to ½ hour before serving, whereas desserts like mousse and custard can be added up to 2 hours before serving. This chapter will provide the procedures used to create three different variations of a standard-style dessert cup, as well as an orange and a swan dessert cup.

STANDARD-STYLE DESSERT CUPS

This chapter provides the procedures used to make solid-colored standard-style dessert cups. The various techniques used to create multicolored blown sugar are described in chapter 10. Always practice on solid-colored sugar-blown pieces before attempting to use multicolored sugar. I use pink- and violet-colored sugar for the first two standard-style dessert cups, and green- and white-colored sugar for the third standard-style dessert cup.

PREPARING THE SUGAR

Using the procedure described in chapter 3, fully aerate a 7-inch disk of precooked sugar. The choice of color is optional. When the sugar is fully aerated, form it into the rectangular building shape. Using scissors, divide the sugar rectangle in half and remove a 1½-inch-diameter ball from each half. Individually form all four pieces of sugar into the rectangular building shape. Place one of the larger and both of the smaller sugar rectangles on a fabric work rack away from the heat. Place the other large sugar rectangle at the center of the fabric work rack under the infrared heat. Using a four-bulb heating system, it will take approximately 7 minutes to prepare the sugar.

STYLE (1)

1. Heat the sugar rectangle until a uniform gloss covers its surface completely. Lengthen the rectangle by pulling each end approximately half the length of the original rectangle and fold the ends back carefully, meeting at the center of the rectangle, as described in the building process. Repeat the building process, always waiting for a high-gloss shine to appear on the sugar surface before folding the sugar. As the sugar approaches the blowing-ready temperature, fold the ends back to the center without lengthening the rectangle. Continue to build the sugar until it is folded into a tight mass. Then quickly form the

sugar into a blowing-ready ball. Using a four-bulb heating system, it will take approximately 3 minutes to prepare the sugar into a blowing-ready ball.

2. Attach the blowpipe to the sugar. I usually use a 10-millimeter blowpipe to make a standard-style dessert cup.

3. Following the procedures described in the blowing process of the sphere, blow softly while rotating the blowpipe and sugar evenly until the air chamber has filled the ball and it has expanded into a small sphere approximately 2 inches in diameter. Pull the sphere away carefully from the end of the blowpipe to create a margin between the end of the blowpipe and the start of the sphere. Continue to rotate and blow softly until the sugar has expanded to approximately a 3-inch sphere. It will take approximately 3½ minutes to complete this step.

4. Using the procedures described in the cooling process, allow the sphere to cool in front of a fan set on high.

5. After the sphere is cooled completely, split the sphere horizontally in half. Allow the edges of both halves to cool in front of a fan and place the half not attached to the blowpipe on a fabric work rack away from the heat. Carefully remove the blowpipe from the sugar, and after cooling the bottom of the sphere, place it with the other half on a fabric work rack away from the heat. Each half of the sphere will be used to make a dessert cup.

6. Using the flame of an alcohol burner, heat a spot at the edge of one of the half-spheres for a couple of seconds (do not overheat). When the sugar is soft, use your finger to press the edge outward carefully to create a ruffle (see fig. 10–6). The best method for finishing this technique is to envision the edge of the half sphere as a clock face. Make the first ruffle at the twelve o'clock position, and the second ruffle at the six o'clock position. Stop to cool the edge in front of a fan.

After the edge has cooled, make the next ruffle at the three o'clock position, then across at the nine o'clock position, and again allow the edge to cool. Continue the procedure until the edge is ruffled completely (see fig. 10–7).

7. Allow the ruffled edge to cool completely in front of a fan. Using the flame of an alcohol burner, heat a spot approximately ½ inch from the very bottom of the sphere. Heat the sugar quickly (a few seconds) and be careful not to overheat. (It is better to have to heat the sugar a second time if necessary than to overheat it on the first attempt.)When the sugar is soft, use the lightly oiled end of the large solid-glass manipulator to push the soft sugar slowly and carefully from the inside of the half sphere, creating a small knob (fig. 11–1). Allow the knob to cool in front of a fan and repeat the procedure twice, carefully placing the other two knobs so they create a tripod (C-12).

STYLE (2)

1. Place the two small sugar rectangles at the center of the fabric work rack under the infrared heat. Do not allow the sugar to touch. Build the sugars until they are uniformly soft, using the procedures described in chapter 3. When the sugar is soft, form both pieces into cylinders approximately 2 inches long and ½ inch in diameter.

2. Slowly and carefully pull each of the sugar cylinders into uniformly thin cords approximately 15 inches long. Using scissors, cut the cord in half and place the cords together side by side on the fabric work rack. Then pinch the ends of the cords and twist them into an even coil approximately 24 inches long (see fig. 4–11).

3. Using scissors, remove a 12-inch length of coil, and starting at one end, wind the coil into a flat circle approximately 2 inches in diameter. Place the circled coil away from the heat on top of the wooden frame at the edge of the fabric work rack until it is cool.

4. When the circled coil is cooled completely, heat the center of the circled coil over the flame of an alcohol burner, and attach the bottom of the half sphere left over from Style (1) (step 1) to the circled coil. Allow the base and top to cool by carefully holding it in front of a fan set on high. If necessary, adjust the top to keep the edge of the top parallel with the base.

5. Slowly pull the remainder of the coil into a uniformly thin coil approximately ⅛ inch in diameter and at least 12 inches long. Measure the top edge of the cup with a string, and using scissors, remove a length of coil the same length as the string. Form the coil into a circle on the fabric work rack and press the ends together smoothly. While the sugar is still soft, yet firm enough to handle, carefully set the coil on the edge of the half-sphere and very slightly push the coil down onto the edge (C-12). To ensure a strong bond, heat the end of a pencil-thick stick of sugar and tack the bottom inside edge of the coil to the inside of the bowl every 90 degrees along the circumference of the edge.

STYLE (3)

1. Place the last sugar rectangle under the infrared heat. Gradually build the sugar up to the blowing-ready temperature. When the sugar reaches the blowing-ready temperature, form the sugar into a blowing-ready ball. Using a four-bulb heating system, it will take approximately 9 minutes to prepare the sugar into a blowing-ready ball.

2. Attach the blowpipe to the sugar. I usually use a 10-millimeter blowpipe for the standard-style dessert cup.

3. Following the procedures described in the blowing process of the sphere, blow softly while rotating the blowpipe and sugar evenly, until the air chamber has filled the ball and it has expanded into a sphere approximately 2 inches in diameter. Carefully pull the sphere away from the end of the blowpipe to create a margin between the end of the blowpipe and the start of the sphere. Con-

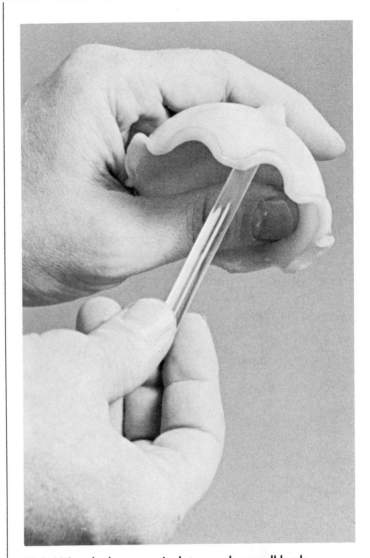

11-1. Using the large manipulator, push a small knob out the bottom of the half sphere.

11-2. Horizontally split away three-fourths of the sphere.

11-3. Attach the top of the sphere's smaller section to the bottom of the larger section.

tinue to rotate and blow softly until the sphere has expanded to approximately a 3½-inch-diameter sphere. Be sure to maintain the margin between blowpipe and sphere. It will take approximately 4 minutes to complete this step.

4. Using the procedures described in the cooling process, allow the sphere to cool in front of a fan set on high.

5. After the sphere is cooled completely, horizontally split the sphere. Remove three-fourths of the sphere, leaving one-fourth of the sphere attached to the blowpipe (fig. 11–2). Allow the edges of both parts of the sphere to cool in front of a fan and place the part of the sphere not attached to the blowpipe on a fabric work rack away from the heat. Carefully remove the blowpipe from the sugar, making sure to leave at least a ½-inch margin at the bottom of the sphere. After cooling the bottom of the sphere, place it on a fabric work rack away from the heat.

6. Using the flame of an alcohol burner, heat the top edge of the margin on the smaller part of the split sphere, and attach the bottom of the larger part of the split sphere on top of the margin (fig. 11–3). Allow both parts to cool by holding them carefully in front of a fan. If necessary, adjust the top half of the dessert cup to keep the edge of the top parallel with the edge on the bottom half.

7. Using the procedures described in chapter 3, prepare an 8-inch disk of precooked sugar to the pulling-ready state. Use a small amount of green food coloring to color the sugar. When the sugar is at the pulling-ready temperature, pull eight leaves from the sugar (see chapter 4). Each leaf should be approximately 2 inches wide and 3 inches long. Curve the last one-third of each leaf on the stem's end of the leaf into a hook (fig. 11–4).

8. Heat the stems of the leaves over the flame of an alcohol burner and attach the stems ½ inch below the top edge on the inside of the top half of the dessert cup. Attach the leaves evenly along the

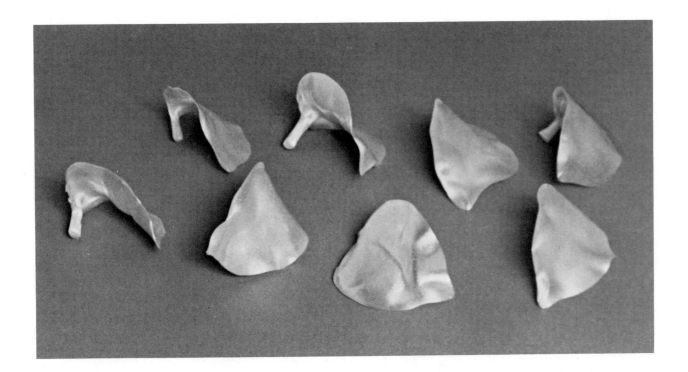

circumference of the top edge (C-12). This style of dessert cup is especially suited for a dessert of fresh berries or fruit.

11-4. Curve the stem end of the leaves into a hook.

ORANGE DESSERT CUP

Note: A more detailed description and photographs of the procedures used to make an orange can be found in chapter 5.

1. Using the procedures described in chapter 3, separately but simultaneously fully aerate a 7-inch and a 4-inch disk of precooked sugar. Color the 7-inch disk by using a small amount of orange food coloring, and color the 4-inch disk by using a small amount of green food coloring. Two large oranges approximately 4 inches in diameter can be made from a 7-inch disk of sugar, and fifteen citrus leaves 1¼ inches wide and 3 inches long can be pulled from a 4-inch disk of sugar. When the sugar is fully aerated, form the green-colored sugar into the rectangular building shape and place it on a fabric work rack away from the heat. Using scissors, divide the orange-colored sugar in half, and form each piece into the rectangular building shape. Place one of the rectangles on a

fabric work rack away from the heat and place the other at the center of the fabric work rack under the infrared heat. Using a four-bulb heating system, it will take approximately 9 minutes to prepare the sugar.

2. Build the sugar rectangle into a blowing-ready ball. Using a four-bulb heating system, it should take approximately 4 minutes to complete this step.

3. Attach the blowpipe to the sugar. I usually use a 13-millimeter blowpipe to make an orange.

4. Blow softly while rotating the blowpipe and sugar evenly until the air chamber has filled the ball and it has expanded into a small sphere approximately 2 inches in diameter. Carefully pull the sphere away from the end of the blowpipe to create a margin between the end of the blowpipe and the start of the sphere. Continue to rotate and blow softly until the sugar has expanded to a 4-inch sphere. It will take approximately 4 minutes to complete this step.

5. Cool the orange in front of a fan set on high. When the orange is cooled completely, split it in half horizontally. Allow the edges of both halves to cool in front of a fan and place the half not attached to the blowpipe on a fabric work rack away from the heat. Carefully remove the blowpipe from the sugar and cool the bottom of the orange in front of a fan.

6. Attach the bottom of the orange half that was closest to the blowpipe to a poured-sugar base.

7. Place the green-colored sugar rectangle at the center of the fabric work rack under the infrared heat. Turn the sugar over every 60 seconds to maintain an even temperature. When the sugar is heated to the pulling-ready temperature, pull an orange stem and two citrus leaves approximately 1 inch wide and 3 inches long (see chapter 4).

8. Heat the end of the orange stem over the flame of an alcohol burner and attach it to the top of the top half of the orange. Heat the stems of the leaves over an alcohol burner and attach them at the bottom of the stem (C-13).

SWAN DESSERT CUP

Note: A more detailed description and photographs of the procedures used to make a swan can be found in chapter 9.

1. Using the procedures described in chapter 3, prepare a 4-inch disk of precooked sugar into the blowing-ready cylindrical shape. The swan's white color is achieved by aerating to opacity. No food coloring is necessary. A 4-inch disk of sugar is used to make a swan's body, approximately 5 inches long and 2½ inches in diameter. Using a four-bulb heating system, it will take approximately 5 minutes to prepare the sugar into a blowing-ready cylinder.

2. Attach the blowpipe to the sugar. I usually use a 10-millimeter blowpipe to make the swan dessert cup.

3. Blow softly while rotating the blowpipe and sugar evenly until the air chamber starts to expand at the end of the blowpipe. While you are blowing, use your fingers to restrict the air chamber's outward expansion. This will allow the air chamber to move forward through the cylinder. Continue to rotate while blowing softly until the air chamber has filled two-thirds of the cylinder. It will take approximately 3 minutes to complete this step.

4. With your fingertips, gently form the solid sugar at the end of the cylinder into a soft point, and bend it upward perpendicular to the blown section (see fig. 9–1). Do not squeeze or excessively handle the solid-sugar end.

5. Carefully pull the air chamber into an oval shape (see fig. 9–2). Immediately after pulling, blow softly until all the creases and fingermarks are removed from the blown surface.

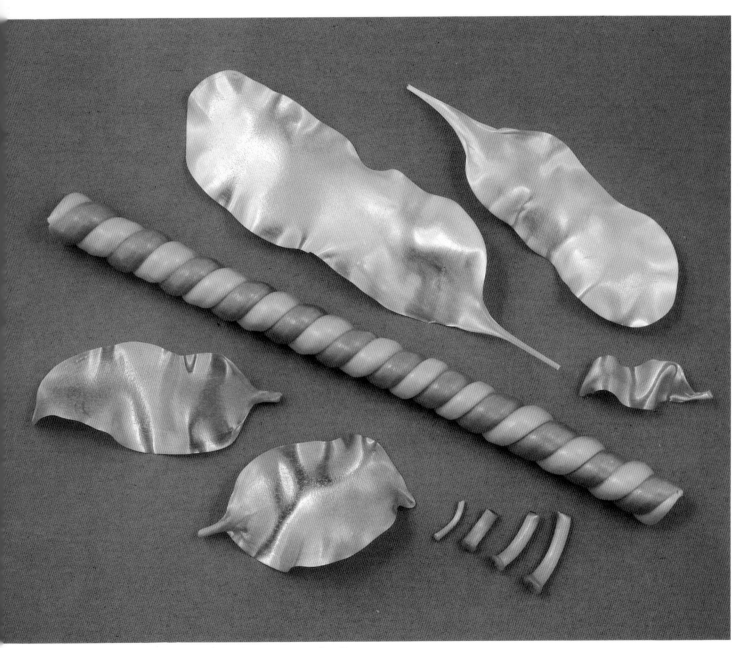

C-1. Fruit leaves, swan feathers, fruit stems, and coil.

C-2. The ribbon loop and ribbon bow.

C-3. The orange and banana.

C-4. The lemon, grape, strawberry, banana, pear, green apple, orange, and red apple.

C-5. The fruit bowl.

C-6. The dolphin centerpiece.

C-7. The large vase.

C-8. The swan centerpiece.

C-9. The preblowing shapes for multicolored blown sugar.

C-10. Single-color and multicolored ornament hooks.

C-11. Three styles of Christmas ornaments.

C-12. The standard-style dessert cups.

C-13. The swan and orange dessert cups.

C-14. The standard-style and strawberry candy dishes.

C-15. The free-hand and mold-blown wine glasses.

C-16. The parts of the rose.

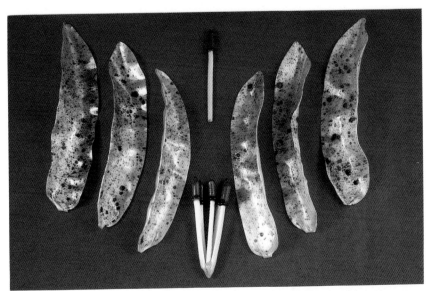

C-17. The parts of the lily.

C-18. The parts of the tulip.

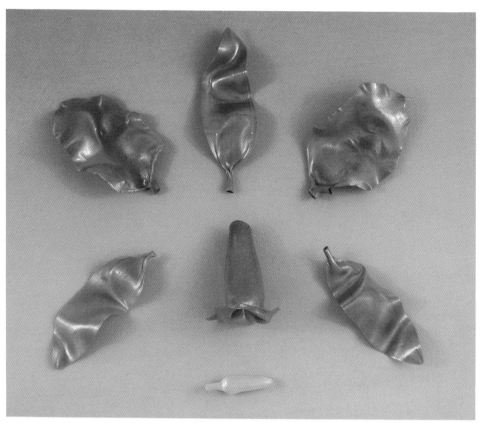

C-19. The parts of the orchid.

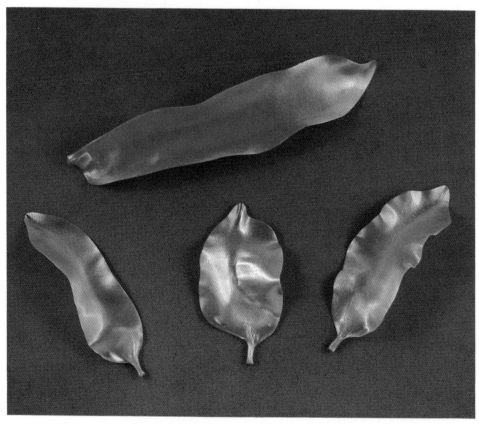

C-20. Flower leaves: lily *(bottom left)*; tulip *(bottom center)*; rose *(bottom right)*; orchid *(top)*.

C-21. The flowers
and large vase.

C-22. Blown- and pulled-sugar candies.

6. Finish the blowing process with the swan at the center of a fabric work rack away from the heat, placed directly in front of a fan set on medium. With one hand holding the blowpipe and the other holding the tip of the solid sugar while blowing, continue to alternate equally between blowing and pulling the air chamber, until the body is approximately 5 inches long and 2½ inches in diameter. It will take approximately 2½ minutes to complete this step.

7. With one hand lightly holding the base of the solid sugar, and the other holding at the top, slowly and evenly pull the solid sugar up perpendicular and proportionate to the blown body, and carefully bend it into the swan's familiar curve (see fig. 9–3). I try to keep the length of the swan's neck, after it is curved, the same length as the swan's body. Additional blowing should be done only to remove unwanted indentations, such as fingermarks.

8. Allow the swan to cool in front of a fan set on high. Be sure to maintain symmetry between the swan's neck and body.

9. Slowly heat the last inch of the swan's neck over the flame of an alcohol burner. To prevent overheating, move the sugar in and out of the flame until the sugar is soft enough to mold with your fingers. Quickly form the head and the beak, using scissors to remove any excess sugar.

10. Cool the head in front of a fan and remove the blowpipe from the sugar. Immediately after removing the blowpipe, attach the swan's bottom to a poured-sugar base.

11. Allow the swan to cool on the base by holding it carefully in front of a fan. When the sugar is cooled completely and the swan is firmly attached to the base, heat a spot at the top of the swan's body over the flame of an alcohol burner for a couple seconds. Do not overheat. Wait 30 seconds, then using your fingers, carefully and slowly press a depression, approximately 2 inches deep and 2 inches in diameter, into the

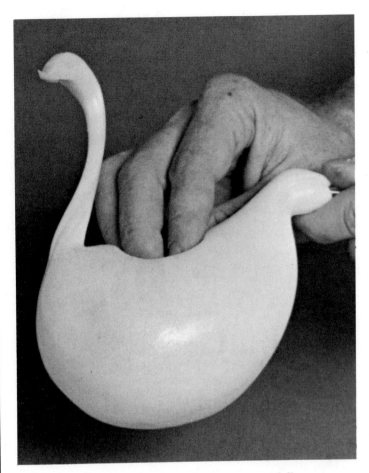

11-5. Use your fingers to form a depression carefully into the swan's back.

swan's body (fig. 11–5). The dessert is added later into this depression. Allow the top of the swan to cool by holding it in front of a fan, and when completely cooled, place it on a fabric work rack away from the heat.

12. Using the procedures described in chapter 3, prepare a 4-inch disk of precooked sugar to a white-colored pulling-ready state. This sugar is used to pull the swan's side and tail feathers. Using a four-bulb heating system, it will take approximately 8 minutes to prepare the sugar into a pulling-ready state.

13. Using the sugar-pulling procedures used to make a swan feather, pull out eight side feathers, each approximately 4 inches long and 1½ inches wide (C-1). As they are completed, place the feathers on a fabric work rack away from the heat.

14. Using the sugar-pulling procedures, pull out three tail feathers, each approximately 2 inches long and 1 inch wide (C-1). Place the tail feathers with the side feathers as they are completed.

15. Heat the bottom edge of one of the tail feathers over the flame of an alcohol burner. Do not overheat. Attach the feather to the top of the swan's rear (see fig. 9–6). Attach the other two tail feathers on both sides of the first tail feather and slightly overlapping its edge.

16. Starting on the top at one side of the swan's rear, (see fig. 9–5), evenly attach the side feathers to the swan's body, four feathers per side. When completed, allow the feathers to cool by placing the swan head-first in front of a fan set at low speed.

Assemble the side feathers, allowing for easy access to the depression on the top of the swan (C-13). I usually fill the swan dessert cup with a chocolate mousse, using a pastry bag to pipe in the mousse.

CHAPTER 12

CANDY DISHES

A sugar-blown candy dish provides a unique and elegant method for displaying all types of confections. The candy dish, like the dessert cup, can be colored, flavored, and shaped to accent the ingredients. The candy dishes make excellent gifts for holidays such as Valentine's Day, Easter, and Christmas. They can add a beautiful finishing touch to a banquet table, a wedding table, or a fine restaurant's dessert cart. This chapter will provide the procedures used to make two styles of candy dishes: a standard-style white-colored sugar cup usually filled with assorted chocolates, and a large strawberry filled with small strawberry-shaped candies.

STANDARD-STYLE CANDY DISH

1. Using the procedures described in chapter 3, fully aerate an 8-inch disk of precooked sugar. The sugar is colored white by aerating to opacity. No food coloring is necessary. When the sugar is fully aerated, use scissors to divide the sugar in half. Form each piece into the rectangular building shape, and place one of the sugar rectangles on a fabric work rack away from the heat and the other at the center of the fabric work rack under the infrared heat. Using a four-bulb heating system, it will take approximately 8 minutes to fully aerate the sugar.

2. Heat the sugar rectangle until a uniform gloss covers its surface completely. Lengthen the rectangle by pulling each end approximately half the length of the original rectangle, and carefully fold the ends back to the center of the rectangle, as described in the building process. Repeat the building process, always waiting for the high-gloss shine to cover the sugar's surface completely before folding the sugar. As the sugar approaches the blowing-ready temperature, fold the ends back to the center without lengthening the rectangle. Continue to build the sugar until it is folded into a tight mass. Then quickly form the sugar into a blowing-ready ball. Using a four-bulb heating system, it will take approximately 3½ minutes to prepare the sugar into a blowing-ready ball.

3. Attach the blowpipe to the sugar. I usually use a 14-millimeter blowpipe to make the standard-style candy dish.

4. Following the procedures described in the blowing process of the sphere, blow softly while rotating the blowpipe and sugar evenly, until the air chamber has filled the ball and it has expanded into a small sphere approximately 2 inches in diameter. Carefully pull the sphere away from the blowpipe to create a margin between the end of the blowpipe and the start of the sphere. Continue to rotate and blow softly

12-1. The parts of the standard candy dish.

until the sphere has expanded to approximately a 4½-inch-diameter sphere. It will take approximately 5 minutes to complete this step.

5. Using the procedures described in the cooling process, allow the sphere to cool in front of a fan set on high.

6. When the sphere is cooled completely, split the sphere in half horizontally. Allow the edges of both halves to cool in front of a fan and place the half not attached to the blowpipe on a fabric work rack away from the heat. Carefully remove the blowpipe from the sugar and cool the bottom of the sphere in front of a fan. When removing the blowpipe, be sure to leave approximately ¼ inch of the margin at the bottom of the other half, which is the bottom of the candy dish.

7. Attach the bottom half of the sphere to a poured-sugar base and allow the sugar to cool in front of a fan. Make sure the top edge of the bottom half of the sphere is parallel to the poured-sugar base.

8. Place the other sugar rectangle at the center of the fabric work rack under the infrared heat. To

maintain an even temperature while heating, turn the sugar over every 60 seconds. When the sugar reaches the pulling-ready temperature, pull approximately fifteen ribbon loops, each ribbon loop approximately 1 inch long and 1 inch wide (fig. 12–1). As the ribbon loops are completed, place them on a fabric work rack away from the heat. Using a four-bulb heating system, it will take approximately 4 minutes to heat the sugar to the pulling-ready temperature.

9. Using scissors, remove a ball of sugar approximately 1 inch in diameter, and make a circular-coiled ornament hook approximately 1/8 inch thick and 3/8 inch in diameter. Allow the hook to cool by placing it on the wooden frame at the edge of the fabric work rack (fig. 12–1).

10. Heat the end of the ribbon loops over the flame of an alcohol burner and attach them evenly along the top edge of the bottom half of the sphere (fig. 12–2). Allow the sugar to cool by holding it carefully in front of a fan. Heat the bottom of the ornament hook over the alcohol burner, attach it at the top and center of the top half of the sphere, and allow the sugar to cool.

The candy is added to the bottom of the candy dish, using small individual paper cups to separate the candies. I usually use a variety of chocolate candies to fill this candy dish. Place the top half of the candy dish onto the bottom half and it is ready for presentation (C-14).

STRAWBERRY CANDY DISH

1. Place a 6-inch and a 4-inch disk of precooked sugar on the fabric work rack under the infrared heat. Do not allow the disks to touch. Using the procedures described in chapter 3, separately but simultaneously aerate the sugar disks. Use a little red food coloring to color the 6-inch disk of sugar and use a little green food coloring to color the 4-inch disk of sugar. Alternate between reheating and aerating the sugar until both disks are fully aerated. After the sugar is aerated, individually form each piece of sugar into the rectan-

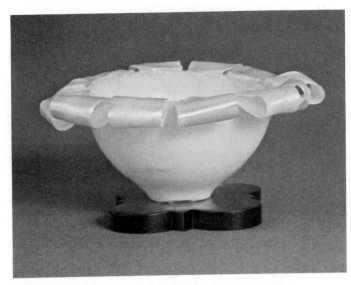

12-2. Attach the ribbon loops along the edge of the half sphere.

gular building shape. Place the green-colored rectangle on a fabric work rack away from the heat and place the red-colored rectangle at the center of the fabric work rack under the infrared heat. Using a four-bulb heating system, it will take approximately 9 minutes to fully aerate the two disks of sugar.

2. Heat the sugar rectangle until a uniform gloss covers its surface completely. Lengthen the rectangle by pulling each end approximately half the length of the original rectangle, and carefully fold the ends back to the center of the rectangle, as described in the building process. Repeat the building process, always waiting for the high-gloss shine to cover the sugar's surface completely before folding the sugar. As the sugar approaches the blowing-ready temperature, fold the ends back to the center without lengthening the rectangle. Continue to fold the sugar until it is folded into a tight mass. Then quickly form the sugar into a blowing-ready ball. Using a four-bulb heating system, it will take approximately 4 minutes to prepare the sugar into a blowing-ready ball.

3. Attach the blowpipe to the sugar. I usually use a 13-millimeter blowpipe to make the strawberry candy dish.

4. Following the procedures described in the blowing process of the sphere, blow softly while rotating the blowpipe and sugar evenly, until the air chamber has filled two-thirds of the ball. With your fingertips, gently pull the last half of the ball into a soft point, and carefully pull the sphere away from the end of the blowpipe to create a margin between the end of the blowpipe and the start of the sphere. It will take approximately 3 minutes to complete this step.

5. Maintain the strawberry's tapered end by using your hands to restrict the outward expansion at the pointed end of the sphere while blowing. Continue to rotate and blow softly until the air chamber has penetrated through to the point, and the strawberry has expanded to approxi-

mately 4½ inches in diameter at the top, and 5 inches long, tapering to a point at the bottom (fig. 12–3). It should take approximately 4 minutes to complete the blowing process.

6. Using the procedures described in the cooling process, allow the strawberry to cool in front of a fan set on high.

7. To simulate the seeds from the strawberry, carefully use the point of a paring knife heated over the flame of an alcohol burner to make tiny indentations randomly across the strawberry's surface, until they are evenly distributed. Stop periodically to cool the strawberry in front of a fan to prevent the surface from collapsing. Using a small stiff-bristled paintbrush, add a touch of green or brown food coloring into the indentations.

8. Horizontally split the strawberry 1 inch below the top edge. Allow the edges of both sections to cool in front of a fan and place the bottom of the strawberry on a fabric work rack away from the heat. Carefully remove the blowpipe from the sugar, and after cooling the top section of the strawberry, place it on a fabric work rack away from the heat.

9. Attach the point at the bottom of the strawberry to a poured-sugar base. Allow the sugar to cool by holding it carefully in front of a fan. Be sure the top edge of the bottom of the strawberry is parallel to the poured-sugar base. When the sugar is cooled completely, place the sugar on a fabric work rack away from the heat.

10. Place the green-colored rectangle at the center of the fabric work rack under the infrared heat. To maintain an even temperature while heating, turn the sugar over every 60 seconds. When the sugar reaches the pulling-ready temperature, use the sugar-pulling procedures to pull seven large strawberry leaves, each approximately 2½ inches long and ½ inch wide. As the leaves are completed, place them on a fabric work rack away from the heat (fig. 12–4). Using a four-bulb

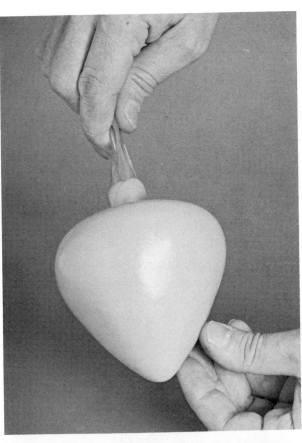

12-3. The finished blowing process
of the large strawberry.

12-4. The parts of the strawberry candy dish.

heating system, it should take approximately 4 minutes to heat the sugar to the pulling-ready temperature.

11. Using scissors, remove a ball of sugar approximately ½ inch in diameter, and with your fingers, flatten and spread the ball into a thin circle approximately ¾ inch in diameter. Place the circle on a fabric work rack away from the heat (fig. 12–4), and using scissors, remove another small ball of sugar and pull it into a thin cord approximately ⅟₁₆ inch in diameter. Using scissors, remove a ½-inch length of cord, bend it slightly to resemble a strawberry stem, and place it on a fabric work rack away from the heat (fig. 12–4).

12. Heat the bottom edge of the thin circle over the flame of an alcohol burner and attach it to the center at the top of the strawberry. Press the edges of the circle firmly to the top of the strawberry to ensure a strong and permanent bond. Heat the stem end of the strawberry leaves over the alcohol burner and attach them evenly around the top of the strawberry. Heat the end of the strawberry stem and attach it to the center at the top of the strawberry. For the best results, use a natural strawberry or a photograph as a model. The strawberry candy dish (C-14) is filled with small sugar-blown strawberry-shaped candies. Instructions for making strawberry-shaped candies are in chapter 16.

CHAPTER 13

SUGAR GLASSES

Sugar-blown wine glasses can be as delicate, beautiful, and varied in style as glass-blown wine glasses, and the sugar-blown wine glasses can hold their ingredients. The sugar wine glass is made using thin-walled sugar, 1/16-inch thick, at the top of the sugar-blown vessel, giving the glass a delicate appearance. The wall thickness gradually increases to 1/8-inch thick at the bottom of the vessel, which allows the wine glass to hold its ingredients. Two sugar wine glasses easily can be used to consume the contents of a bottle of wine. This chapter will provide the procedures used to make two different glass styles: a free-hand champagne glass and a mold-blown wine glass. Both styles are made using unaerated, transparent sugar, colored during the cooking process. (Poured-sugar bases are used to make the vessels and the bottoms of sugar-blown wine glasses. See *Small Base* and *Thick Base* in chapter 2 for a description of how to make bases for sugar-blown wine glasses.)

The stems for the sugar glasses can be made from pulled sugar, nougatine, pastillage, metal, wood, or glass. This chapter uses glass-pulled Pyrex rods for the glass stems. I prefer the glass stems because they are reusable and the glass's transparency adds to the illusion of the sugar-blown glasses. Both the large and the small solid-glass manipulators in the standard blowpipe set can be used for the glass stems.

Note: Blowing transparent sugar allows you to see the air chamber as it expands and moves through the sugar. The air chamber should expand evenly through the sugar, producing an even wall thickness. If one side of the sugar becomes thinner than the other side while blowing, use your hands to restrict the outward expansion of the thinner side until the wall thickness equalizes. Restrict the outward expansion by changing from hand to hand while continuing to rotate the blowpipe and sugar. Slow and even blowing is the best way to maintain a uniform wall thickness.

FREE-HAND CHAMPAGNE GLASS

1. Place a thick, circular poured-sugar base approximately 3 inches in diameter and 7/8 inch thick at the center of the fabric work rack under the infrared heat (fig. 13–1). To maintain an even temperature in the sugar while heating, turn the sugar over every 2 minutes. As the sugar softens, periodically use your fingers to press the perimeter of the sugar base into a compact mass at the center of the fabric work rack. Heat the sugar until it reaches the blowing-ready temperature and form it into a blowing-ready ball. Attach the blowpipe

13-1. Place the thick poured-sugar disk at the center of the fabric work rack.

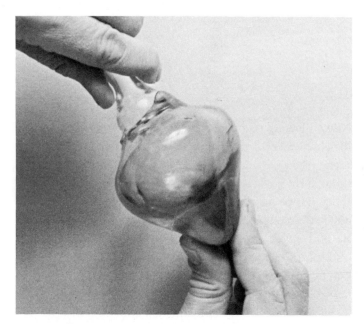

13-2. Form the solid sugar at the end of the ball into a soft point.

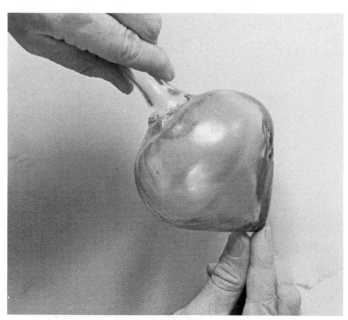

13-3. The finished blowing process of the squat sphere.

to the sugar. I usually use a 22-millimeter blow-pipe to make the free-hand champagne glass. Using a four-bulb heating system, it will take approximately 15 minutes to heat the thick sugar base to a blowing-ready ball.

2. Using the procedures in the blowing process of the sphere, blow softly while rotating the blow-pipe and sugar evenly, until the air chamber has penetrated two-thirds of the ball. Make sure the air chamber moves evenly through the sugar. Carefully pull the solid sugar at the end of the ball into a soft point (fig. 13–2). Maintaining a margin between the end of the blowpipe and the start of the blown ball is not required because the ball is split in half after it is completed and only the half farthest from the blowpipe is used. It will take approximately 4 minutes to complete this step.

3. While using your hands to restrict the outward expansion of the end of the ball, continue to rotate and blow softly until the sugar has expanded to a small sphere approximately 2½ inches in diameter. Restricting the outward expansion of the end of the ball will allow the sugar's wall thickness at the point of the ball (bottom of vessel) to remain twice as thick as the sugar in the middle of the ball (top edge of vessel). The wall thickness at the bottom will become thinner gradually until it reaches the middle. This result is best achieved by blowing and rotating slowly and uniformly, while evenly restricting the end of the ball.

4. Finish the blowing process, holding the blowpipe and sugar upward, perpendicular to the ground. Continue to rotate and blow softly while restricting the outward expansion at the end of the ball until the sphere expands into a squat sphere approximately 4 inches in diameter (horizontally) with a slight point at the bottom of the ball (fig. 13–3). It will take approximately 4 minutes to complete the blowing process.

5. Using the procedures described in the cooling process, cool the sugar in front of a fan set on high.

6. After the sugar is cooled completely, split the squat sphere in half horizontally. Allow the edge on the pointed bottom of the split sphere to cool in front of a fan and place it on a fabric work rack away from the heat.

   Note: If the wall thickness at the bottom of the vessel is not at least ⅛ inch thick, attach a small poured-sugar base approximately 1 inch in diameter and ¼ inch thick to the bottom of the vessel.

7. Heat one of the ends of the glass stem over the flame of an alcohol burner for approximately 15 seconds. Do not overheat. If the stem caramelizes the sugar when contact is made, carefully clean the end of the stem, and allow the stem to cool for approximately 30 seconds before reattaching. Slowly and carefully attach the stem to the bottom of the vessel by turning while gently pushing the stem into the bottom at least ⅛ inch deep (fig. 13–4). Allow the sugar to cool by carefully holding it in front of a fan. Make sure the stem extends in a straight line from the middle of the bottom of the vessel.

8. After the sugar is cooled completely and the stem is attached securely, heat the bottom end of the stem over the flame of an alcohol burner for 15 seconds and attach it to the center of a small poured-sugar base approximately 3½ inches in diameter and ¼ inch thick (fig. 13–5). Attach the stem to the base approximately ⅛ inch deep, using the same technique as used for attaching the top of the vessel. Allow the glass to cool completely by carefully holding it in front of a fan. Make sure the top edge of the vessel is parallel to the poured-sugar base (C-15).

MOLD-BLOWN WINE GLASS

Note: The molds used to make sugar-blown glasses can be made of plastic or ceramic. For the best results, the wall thickness of a plastic mold should be at least ¹⁄₃₂ inch thick and the wall thickness of a ceramic mold should be at least ¼ inch thick. Metal or glass molds should not be used because they con-

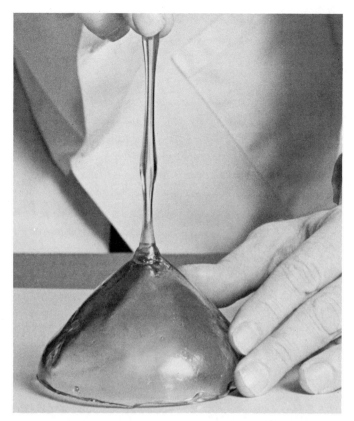

13-4. Attach the stem into the bottom of the half sphere.

13-5. Attach the bottom of the stem into a poured-sugar base.

duct heat too readily. The hot sugar would heat the glass or metal mold quickly, which would cause the sugar to stick. This chapter uses a plastic bell mold to make the sugar wine-glass vessel. Using a mold for blowing the sugar glasses can give the glasses the consistency necessary when more than one glass is required.

Using vegetable oil, lightly oil the inside of the mold and place it away from the heat before the reheating procedures begin. Never allow the mold to get warm before using.

1. Place a thick, circular poured-sugar base approximately 3 inches in diameter and ⅛ inch thick at the center of the fabric work rack under the infrared heat. Using the procedures described in step one of the free-hand champagne glass, heat the sugar by turning it over every 2 minutes until it reaches the blowing-ready temperature. Form the sugar into a blowing-ready ball and attach the blowpipe to the sugar. I generally use a 22-millimeter blowpipe to make the mold-blown wine glass. Using a four-bulb heating system, it will take approximately 15 minutes to complete this step.

2. Using the procedures described in the blowing process of the sphere, blow softly while rotating the blowpipe and sugar evenly, until the air chamber has penetrated one-half of the ball. Make sure the air chamber moves through the sugar evenly. Maintaining a margin between the end of the blowpipe and the start of the blown ball is not necessary because only the bottom half of the ball is required. It will take approximately 3 minutes to complete this step.

3. While using your hands to restrict the outward expansion of the whole ball, continue to rotate

and blow softly until the air chamber has penetrated three-fourths of the ball and the sugar has expanded into a cylinder approximately 5 inches long and 2 inches in diameter. Cool the cylinder by rotating it carefully in front of a fan for approximately 1 minute.

Gently place the end of the cylinder into the lightly oiled mold. Do not push the sugar into the mold. Slowly and evenly rotate the mold, the sugar, and the blowpipe, while blowing softly until the sugar expands and fills the mold (fig. 13–6). Make sure the blowpipe extends on a straight line running through the center of the mold.

4. While holding the blowpipe and the mold carefully, allow the sugar above the mold to cool in front of a fan. After the sugar has cooled, blow softly to make sure the sugar is pressed tightly to the insides of the mold. Carefully remove the sugar from the mold by gently wiggling both the sugar above the mold and the blowpipe until the sugar is removed. Do not turn or twist the blowpipe or sugar when removing (fig. 13–7).

5. Allow the sugar removed from the mold to cool in front of a fan. When the sugar is cooled completely, split the sugar horizontally along the top edge of the mold line. Allow the top edge of the vessel to cool by holding it in front of a fan and then place it on a fabric work rack away from the heat.

6. Using the procedures in steps seven and eight of the free-hand champagne glass, first attach the end of a glass stem to the bottom of the vessel and then attach the end of the stem to a poured-sugar base approximately 3 inches in diameter and ¼ inch thick (C-15).

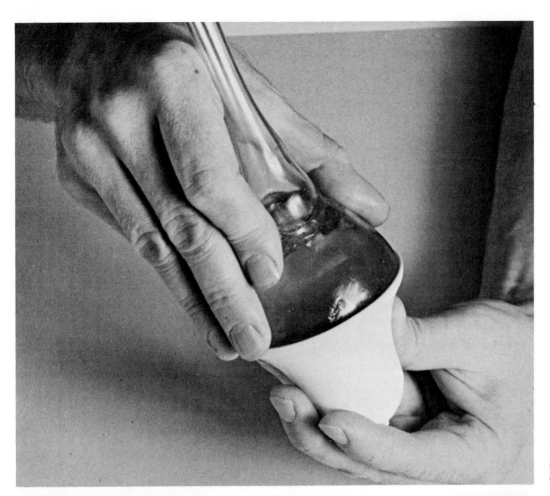

13-6. Blow softly until the sugar fills the mold.

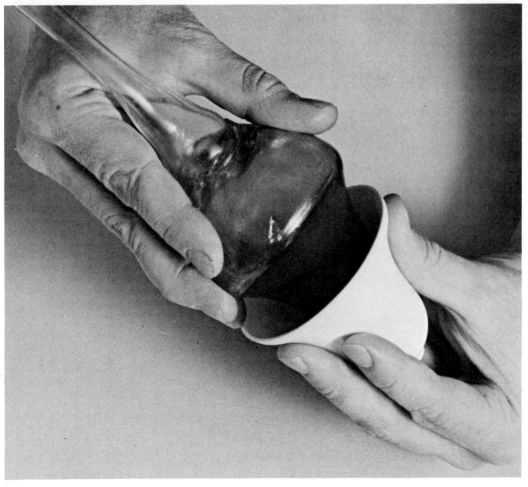

13-7. Gently wiggle the sugar to remove it from the mold.

PART 4

SUGAR PULLING

CHAPTER 14

FLOWERS

Sugar-pulled flowers are the most recognized and replicated creations in sugar work: they are also the most beautiful. Their elegance and fragility reflect the abundance and grace of the natural world. The sugar-pulled flowers can be used in a wide range of displays. Long-stem flowers can be added to a sugar-blown vase to complete a centerpiece or the sugar flowers can be used for decorations on cakes, tortes, desserts, or to highlight a dessert cart in a fine restaurant. The beauty of the sugar-pulled flowers can be enhanced when you create a satinlike finish on the surface of the flower petals.

This chapter will provide the procedures used to make a variation of a rose, lily, tulip, and orchid. The petals used to create these flowers can be altered by softening the sugar under the infrared heat, and pulling, spreading, twisting, or curling the petals to create the various petal shapes of all the natural flowers.

PRELIMINARY PULLING PROCEDURES

When the temperature of the sugar is within the pulling-ready range, fold the sugar in half and pinch down the edge of the fold to form a small band of thin sugar, approximately 1½ inches across and ¾ inch wide (see fig. 4–1). With the bulk of the sugar resting on the fabric work rack, hold the band with your thumbs and index fingers pressed together at

the center, with its tips slightly overlapping the outer edge (see fig. 4–2). Pinch down while uniformly stretching the band until it reaches the desired thickness. The band becomes thinner as it is stretched and can be stretched paper-thin. The thickness of the band once it is stretched will determine the thickness of the pulled sugar.

In my seminars, I have found that beginners achieve their best results by starting to pull the sugar as thick as a banana skin, and after practicing the elementary pulled-sugar shapes and sizes, they can work with thinner sugar.

During the pulling process, always handle the sugar by the edges. Excessive handling will cool the sugar quickly and necessitate repeated reheating, which can cause you to spend more time reheating than pulling.

Be sure to maintain a uniform thickness in your pulled sugar by pulling slowly and gradually from the band. If the piece of pulled sugar is thick at the edges and thin at the center, or vice versa, the sugar was too hot or not at a uniform temperature when pulled. If the piece of pulled sugar is thick at the top (or start) and much thinner at the bottom, the sugar was pulled too quickly or pulled while handling just the top edge and not from the band. If the piece of pulled sugar is thin at the top and thick at the bottom, too much sugar was pulled from the band. Regardless of the size or shape of the intended pulled-sugar piece, always pull evenly from the band

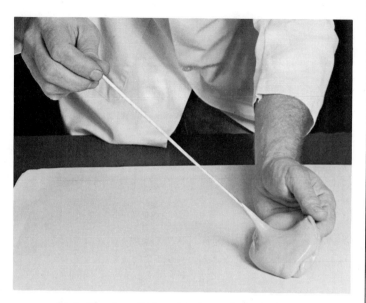

14-1. Slowly pull the wire through the sugar.

until the desired width and length is reached and never pull the piece while handling just the top.

Note: The thin sugar band is the starting point for all pulled-sugar pieces. The sugar must be refolded and a new band stretched for each new piece of sugar pulled.

FLOWER STEMS

The flower stems are made by passing a thin metal rod approximately ⅛ inch in diameter through sugar that is ½ inch thick and completely coats the wire. This chapter uses coat-hanger wire to make the flower stems, although any type of thin metal rod can be used. The temperature of the sugar will determine the thickness of the sugar coating. The wire receives a thin coating of sugar when it is passed through sugar at the highest temperature of the pulling-ready temperature range. As the temperature of the sugar cools, the thickness of the sugar coating increases. When a very thick flower stem is required, the rod can be passed through the sugar twice. If the coating of sugar is too thin, the sugar was too hot. If the coating of sugar breaks apart while passing the wire through the sugar, the sugar was too cold. If the coating of sugar varies in thickness, the sugar was not at a uniform temperature.

The rose and lily stems require a thin coating of sugar, and the tulip and orchid stems require the coating of sugar to be twice as thick. The wire for the rose, lily, and orchid should be bent slightly to duplicate the natural flower stem before the wire is passed through the sugar. The wire for the tulip is left straight. For the best results, use a natural flower or a photograph as a model. To determine the length of the flower stem, measure the sugar vase with the wire before coating it with sugar.

1. Using the procedures described in chapter 3, fully aerate a 12-inch disk of precooked sugar. Color the sugar green. After the sugar has been fully aerated, form the sugar into the rectangular building shape. Evenly spread the center of the sugar rectangle until it is approximately ½ inch

thick. Starting from under the sugar rectangle, slowly push the end of the wire through the center of the sugar approximately 2 inches. While gently holding the end of the wire that was just passed through the sugar, slowly pull the wire through the sugar until it completely covers the wire (fig. 14–1). Using scissors, remove the excess sugar at the bottom of the wire and allow it to cool in front of a fan. After the stem is cooled completely, place it on a fabric work rack away from the heat.

2. Using scissors, remove a small ball of sugar approximately ¾ inch in diameter. Form the sugar into a rose's receptacle, which is the foundation for the sugar petals. The receptacle for the rose is shaped like a diamond (fig. 14–2). The orchid, lily, and tulip receptacles are shaped like cones (fig. 14–2). The receptacle for the orchid is one-half the size of the lily and tulip receptacle. The lily and tulip receptacles are made using the same amount of sugar as the rose receptacle. Join the receptacle to the sugar-coated wire by simultaneously heating the pointed end of the receptacle and the end of the sugar-coated wire over the flame of an alcohol burner. Attach the end of the stem into the point of the receptacle. Press the sugar together firmly to ensure a strong and permanent bond. Allow the stem to cool in front of a fan, and after it is completely cooled, place it on a fabric work rack away from the heat.

Form the sugar into the rectangular building shape and place it on a fabric work rack away from the heat. The remainder of the green sugar will be used to make the leaves for the flowers.

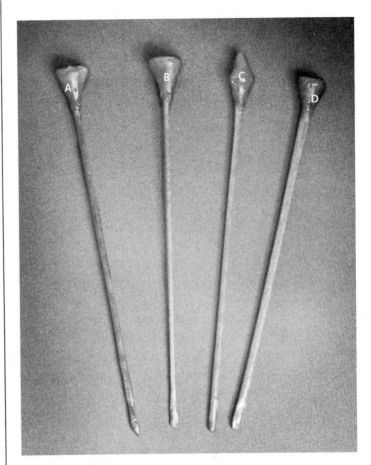

14-2. The lily (A), tulip (B), rose (C), and orchid (D) stems and receptacles.

STYROFOAM FOUNDATIONS

A 6-inch-wide and 4-inch-high styrofoam block is used as the foundation for the flower stems when assembling the flower petals to the receptacle at the top of the flower stem. If large blocks of styrofoam are not available, smaller thicknesses of styrofoam can be glued together to make a block.

Using coat-hanger wire or a similar sized rod,

make a hole approximately 3 inches deep straight down into the center of the styrofoam block. Lightly wrap the last 3 inches at the end of the flower stem with clear plastic wrap and carefully insert it into the hole in the styrofoam.

Note: For the best results, review chapter 4 before attempting to make the flowers.

ROSE

1. Using the procedures described in chapter 3, fully aerate a 10-inch disk of precooked sugar. Color is optional. I use a very small amount of red food coloring to create a light pink color. After the sugar has been fully aerated, turn all but one of the infrared bulbs off. Form the sugar into the rectangular building shape and place it on the fabric work rack away from the heat. Allow the sugar to cool to the pulling-ready temperature. Using a four-bulb heating system, it will take approximately 18 minutes to prepare the sugar into the pulling-ready state.

2. With the nails on your thumb and index finger perpendicular to the band, carefully pinch a small point from the edge of the band approximately ⅛ inch long (top of petal). While pulling just forward of the point, slowly pull an even strip from the band approximately 1½ inches long and ¾ inch wide. Pinch the strip together at the band and remove the strip with scissors. Gently curve the sides of the strip to create a semicircle, and when the petal is completed, place it on a fabric work rack away from the heat. Using the same technique, pull two more petals approximately the same size. Curve the sides of one of the petals exactly like the first petal and, starting at one side, carefully curl the sides of the other petal creating a thin hollow cylinder. As the petals are completed, place them on a fabric work rack away from the heat (C-16). The three petals are used as the center of the rose.

Note: Never attempt the finishing procedures (bending, spreading, twisting, or curling,) on the petals unless the sugar is pliable. Thin pulled-sugar petals are extremely fragile and will cool quickly and become rigid after they have been made. To prevent them from breaking, always heat them directly under an infrared bulb until they are pliable before manipulating them.

3. Using the same procedure as in step 2, carefully pinch a small point from the edge of the band. While pulling just forward of the point, slowly pull an even strip, approximately 1¾ inches long and 1¾ inches wide. Pinch the strip together at the band and remove the strip with scissors. Carefully spread the strip into a circle approximately 1¾ inches in diameter. Shape the center of the petal concave by gently pushing it over your thumb and carefully curl the very edge of the petal back in the same direction as the concave center. Bend back the point at the top of the petal slightly, and curve the petal forward, making it slightly rounded. When the petal is completed, place it on the fabric work rack away from the heat. Using the same procedures, pull two more petals approximately the same size and shape, and place them on a fabric work rack away from the heat (C-16). The three petals interlock their side edges and are attached around the petals at the center.

4. Carefully pinch a small point from the edge of the band and slowly pull an even strip, approximately 2 inches long and 2 inches wide. Pinch the strip together at the band and remove the strip with scissors. Carefully spread the strip into a circle approximately 2 inches in diameter. Using the same procedures as step 3, shape the center of the petal concave, curl back the edges, bend back the point, and curve the petal forward. When the petal is completed, place it on a fabric work rack away from the heat. Using the same procedures, pull four more petals approximately the same size and shape, and place them on a fabric work rack away from the heat (C-16). The five petals interlock their side edges and are attached around the second layer.

14-3. The rose petal assembly.

5. Carefully pinch a small point from the edge of the band and slowly pull an even strip, approximately 2¼ inches long and 2¼ inches wide. Pinch the strip together at the band and remove the strip with scissors. Carefully spread the strip into a circle approximately 2¼ inches in diameter. Shape the center of the petal concave, curl back the edges, bend back the point, and curl the petal forward. When the petal is completed, place it on a fabric work rack away from the heat. Pull six more petals approximately the same size and shape and place them on a fabric work rack away from the heat (C-16). The seven petals interlock their side edges and are attached around the third layer.

Note: A small rose can be made by stopping at the five-petal layer. The seven-petal layer is added only when a large rose is desired.

6. Carefully place the flower stem into the styrofoam base. Using an alcohol burner, heat the bottom edge of the cylindrical center petal and attach it to the point of the rose-stem receptacle (fig. 14–3). Individually heat the bottom edges of the remaining two center petals and attach them to the receptacle on either side of the cylindrical petal with their side edges interlocked around the center (fig. 14–3). Individually heat the bottom edges of the three-petal layer and attach them to the receptacle just below the center petals with their side edges interlocked (fig. 14–3).

Attach the first petal, leaving the edge on one side unattached, creating a crevice. Attach the second petal on the opposite side of the crevice with its side edge overlapping the side edge of the first petal. Attach the third petal with one side interlocking into the crevice of the first petal and the other side edge overlapping the side edge of the second petal.

Allow the petals to cool in place by carefully holding the stem and the styrofoam base together in front of a fan set at medium speed. Individually heat the bottom edges of the five-petal layer and attach them to the receptacle just below the second layer, with their side edges interlocked, using the same procedures as in the three-petal layer (fig. 14–3). Again use the fan to cool the petals in place. Individually heat the bottom edges of the seven-petal layer and attach them to the receptacle just below the third layer, with their side edges interlocked, using the same procedures as in the second layer. Allow the rose to cool in front of a fan, and when cooled completely, place the flower and base away from the heat.

To simulate the thorns on the rose stem, heat the end of a pencil-thick stick of sugar over the flame of an alcohol burner and attach it to the stem. Use your finger to gently press the hot sugar against the stem to ensure a strong and permanent bond. Hold the sugar in place for approximately 30 seconds. Then slowly pull the stick of sugar away from the stem, creating a sharp point. Using scissors, remove the excess sugar from the point, leaving a small, sharp sugar thorn. Using the same process, add the thorns randomly across the surface of the stem.

LILY

1. Using the procedures described in chapter 3, fully aerate an 8-inch disk of precooked sugar. Use a little orange food coloring to color the sugar. After the sugar has been fully aerated, turn all but one of the infrared bulbs off. Form the sugar into the rectangular building shape and place it on a fabric work rack away from the heat. Allow the sugar to cool to the pulling-ready temperature. Using a four-bulb heating system, it will take approximately 15 minutes to prepare the sugar to the pulling-ready state.

2. With the nails on your thumb and index finger perpendicular to the band, carefully pinch a small point from the edge of the band approximately 1/8 inch long (top of petal). While pulling just forward of the point, slowly pull a sharply pointed strip from the edge of the band, approximately 1 1/2 inches wide at the band and 2 inches long, tapering to a point. While maintaining the 1 1/2-inch width, continue to pull the strip slowly from the edge of the band another three inches longer. Pinch the strip together at the band and remove the strip with scissors. Carefully shape the vertical center of the petal slightly concave by curling the petal's side edges evenly. Curve the top of the petal back toward the bottom until the petal is shaped like a hook. When the petal is completed, place it on a fabric work rack away from the heat. Using the same procedures, pull five more petals approximately the same size and shape, and place them on a fabric work rack away from the heat (C–17). The lily is made with six flower petals, three petals per layer.

3. Cover a tabletop with paper and carefully set the lily petals on top of a rolled-up towel covered with fiberglass screening. Place the petals close together but without touching. Dilute some brown food coloring in a small cup, using pure ethyl alcohol or vodka. Dip the end of a small firm-bristle paintbrush into the color. While holding the end of the brush over the petals, use the hand not holding the brush to slap the end of the paintbrush handle lightly. This will place spots randomly across the surface of the petals. Repeat the process until all the petals are spotted

evenly (fig. 14–4). For the best results, use a natural lily or a photograph as a model.

4. Using scissors, remove a 1-inch-diameter ball of orange sugar. Slowly pull the ball into an even cord approximately 1/16 inch thick and at least 12 inches long. Remove seven lengths of cord, each 1½ inches long, with scissors and place the pieces on a fabric work rack away from the heat. The cords are used as the bottom of the stamens, which are attached to the receptacle inside the lily petals. The stamens have a brown cord ½ inch long and ⅛ inch thick attached to their tops. The brown cord can be made two ways: use the procedures described in chapter 3 to prepare a small amount of brown-colored pulling-ready sugar; or use orange-colored sugar, and after the stamens are attached to the lily, the tops of the stamens can be colored using a small paint brush and brown food coloring. The tops of the stamens are attached by simultaneously heating the edges of both parts of the stamen over the flame of an alcohol burner and attaching them. As the stamens are completed, place them on a fabric work rack away from the heat (C-17).

5. Individually heat the bottom edges of three of the petals over the flame of an alcohol burner and attach them evenly along the top edge of the lily stem receptacle (fig. 14–5). Allow the inner petals to cool in place by carefully holding them in front of a fan. Heat the bottom edges of the last three petals and attach them to the top edge of the receptacle, equally overlapping the side edges of the petals on the first layer (fig. 14–5). Allow the outer petals to cool in place by holding them in front of a fan.

6. Using one of the stamens as a foundation, individually heat the ends of the stamens over the flame of an alcohol burner, and attach the ends of the stamens together. Allow the stamens to cool in front of a fan. Then heat the end of the stamens over an alcohol burner and attach it to the center of the receptacle inside the petals (fig. 14–5). Cool the stamens in place by holding the flower in front of a fan.

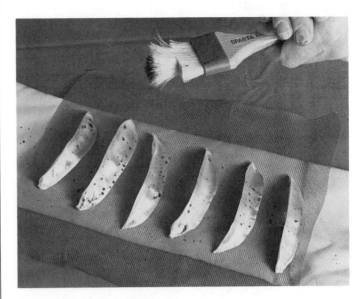

14-4. Evenly spot the lily petals.

14-5. The lily petal assembly.

14-6. The tulip petal assembly.

TULIP

1. Using the procedures described in chapter 3, fully aerate an 8-inch disk of precooked sugar. Color is optional. I use a little yellow food coloring to color the sugar. After the sugar has been fully aerated, turn all but one of the infrared bulbs off. Form the sugar into the rectangular building shape and place it on a fabric work rack away from the heat. Allow the sugar to cool to the pulling-ready temperature. Using a four-bulb heating system, it will take approximately 15 minutes to prepare the sugar into a pulling-ready state.

2. With the nails on your thumb and index finger perpendicular to the band, carefully pinch a small point, approximately ⅛ inch long (top of petal), from the edge of the band. While pulling just forward of the point, slowly pull an even strip from the edge of the band, 1¾ inches wide and 2½ inches long. Pinch the strip together at the band and remove the strip with scissors. Carefully and evenly bend the side edges of the petal, making the petal slightly curved. When the petal is completed, place it on a fabric work rack away from the heat. Using the same procedures, pull five more petals approximately the same size and shape, and place them on a fabric work rack away from the heat (C-18). The tulip is made with six flower petals, three petals per layer.

3. Using scissors, remove a 1-inch-diameter ball of yellow sugar. Slowly pull the ball into an even cord approximately 1/16 inch thick and at least 14 inches long. With scissors, remove eight lengths of cord, each 1¾ inches long. The cords are used as the tulip stamens. Heat the end of the stamens over the flame of an alcohol burner until a small ball of sugar is formed, and as they are completed, place them on a fabric work rack away from the heat (C-18).

4. Individually heat the bottom edges of three of the petals over the flame of an alcohol burner and attach them evenly along the top edge of the tulip-stem receptacle (fig. 14–6). Allow the inner petals to cool in place by carefully holding them in front of a fan. Heat the bottom edges of the last three petals and attach them to the top edge of the receptacle, equally overlapping the side edges of the petals on the first layer (fig. 14–6). Allow the outer petals to cool in place by holding them in front of a fan.

5. Using one of the stamens as a foundation, individually heat the ends of the stamens over an alcohol burner and attach the ends of the stamens together. Allow the stamens to cool in front of a fan and then heat the end of the stamens over an alcohol burner, and attach the end to the center of the receptacle inside the petals (fig. 14–6). Allow the stamens to cool in place by holding the flower in front of a fan.

ORCHID

1. Using the procedures described in chapter 3, fully aerate an 8-inch disk of precooked sugar. Using equal amounts, add a little red and blue food coloring to color the sugar purple. After the sugar has been fully aerated, turn all but one of the infrared bulbs off. Form the sugar into the rectangular building shape and place it on a fabric work rack away from the heat. Allow the sugar to cool to the pulling-ready temperature. Using a four-bulb heating system, it will take approximately 15 minutes to prepare the sugar into the pulling-ready state.

2. With nails on your thumb and index finger perpendicular to the band, carefully pinch a small point, approximately ⅛ inch long (top of petal), from the edge of the band. While pulling just forward of the point, slowly pull an even strip, ¾ inch wide and 2½ inches long, from the edge of the band. Pinch the strip together at the band and remove the strip with scissors. Carefully bend the petal along its length to give it a natural motion. When the petal is completed, place it on a fabric work rack away from the heat. Using the same procedure, pull two more petals approximately the same size and shape, and place them

on a fabric work rack away from the heat (C-19). The three petals, called *sepal petals,* are used as the inner layer of the orchid.

3. Slowly and evenly pull a slightly rounded strip, approximately 2 inches wide and 2¼ inches long (top of petal), from the edge of the band. Pinch the strip together at the band and remove the strip with scissors. Carefully spread the strip into a circle, approximately 2¼ inches in diameter with a slightly rounded point at the top, and then carefully curl the edges of the petal to give it a natural motion. When the petal is completed, place it on a fabric work rack away from the heat. Using the same procedures, pull another petal approximately the same size and shape, and place it on a fabric work rack away from the heat (C-19). The two petals are used for the next layer of the orchid.

4. Slowly and evenly pull a wide strip, approximately 3 inches wide and ½ inch long (top of petal), from the edge of the band. Continue to pull just forward of the strip, and while gradually decreasing the width of the strip, pull the strip until it is 2½ inches long and 1 inch wide at the band. Remove the strip along the edge of the band with scissors. The strip should be shaped like a flat-topped triangle. Evenly curl the last ½ inch at the edge of the base of the triangle back approximately 90 degrees toward the top of the triangle. Carefully wrinkle the entire length of the curled edge, starting at one end, and wrinkling small spots until the entire length is wrinkled. Carefully circle the sides of the triangle together, slightly overlapping their side edges, creating a cone. Using the flame of an alcohol burner, tack both ends and the center of the overlapped edges together firmly. When the petal is completed, place it on a fabric work rack away from the heat (C-19). This petal is called the *lip* or *labellum* and is placed at the center of the orchid.

5. Using scissors, remove approximately a ½-inch-diameter ball of yellow sugar left over from the tulip. Form the sugar into the rectangular building shape, and using the procedures described in chapter 3, gradually build the sugar into a blowing-ready cylinder. Attach a 6-millimeter blowpipe to the sugar and blow softly, while evenly rotating until the air chamber has filled the cylinder and it has expanded into a softly pointed cylinder, approximately 1 inch long and ¼ inch in diameter. Allow the sugar to cool in front of a fan and remove the blowpipe from the sugar. Place the cylinder on a fabric work rack away from the heat (C-19). The blown cylinder is placed inside the lip at the center of the orchid stem receptacle and is called the *column.*

6. Individually heat the bottom edges of the petals from the three-petal layers over the flame of an alcohol burner, and attach them to the side edges at the top of the orchid-stem receptacle, arranged like an airplane propeller (fig. 14–7). Allow the inner petals to cool in place by carefully holding the flower in front of a fan. Individually heat the bottom edges of the two-petal layer over an alcohol burner, and attach them to either side at the top of the receptacle, with the inside edges of the petals overlapping slightly and just forward of the top petal in the three-petal layer (fig. 14–7). Allow the outer petals to cool in place, holding the flower in front of a fan. Heat the bottom end of the orchid's lip over an alcohol burner and attach the lip to the center of the receptacle, bent slightly downward (fig. 14–17). Allow the lip to cool in place by holding the flower in front of a fan. Heat the end of the column that was nearest the blowpipe over an alcohol burner and attach it to the center of the receptacle inside the lip (fig. 14–7). Allow the column to cool in place by holding the flower in front of a fan.

FLOWER LEAVES

Pull a couple of leaves for each of the flower stems, and as they are completed, place them on a fabric work rack away from the heat (C-20). For the best results, use a natural flower leaf or a photograph as a

model. Pull approximately eight extra leaves that can be used to add fullness to the vase.

ASSEMBLING THE FLOWER-AND-VASE CENTERPIECE

Using scissors, remove a ¼-inch-diameter ball of green sugar. Simultaneously heat the edge of the ball and the end of the flower stem over the flame of an alcohol burner and attach them. Allow the end of the stem to cool by holding it in front of a fan. When the sugar is completely cooled, heat the bottom of the sugar ball over an alcohol burner and attach the flower stem into the inside bottom of the vase. Heat the end of a pencil-thick stick of sugar over an alcohol burner and tack the stem firmly to the inside edge at the top of the vase. Repeat this process until all the flower stems are attached into the vase. Heat the stems of the flower leaves with an alcohol burner and attach them to their respective flower stem. Attach the extra leaves along the top inside edge of the vase (C-21).

14-7. The orchid petal assembly.

CHAPTER 15

CANDYCANES

Hand-pulled candycanes can be fun and relatively easy to make, and are a delightful addition to the Christmas holidays. The candycanes can be made with the traditional red and white stripes or they can be made using multicolored stripes. Although one person can perform the procedures required to make the candycanes, a two-person production line is the easiest and most efficient method for making them. In a two-person production line, I use one person to pull the striped cord from the sugar mass while evenly twisting, and the other person, positioned directly behind the first person, removes short lengths of cord with scissors and shapes them into the candycane's familiar hook. This chapter will provide the procedures used to create traditionally striped candycanes using a single-person production line.

1. Using the first mass production recommendation and the procedures described in chapter 3, fully aerate three 10-inch disks or the equivalent of peppermint-flavored precooked sugar. (See step 5 of the *Cooking Process* in chapter 2 for instructions on flavoring the sugar.) White-colored sugar is required, which is achieved by aerating the sugar to opacity and not adding any food coloring. When the sugar is fully aerated, form it into the rectangular building shape and place it on the side of the fabric work rack under the heat of one of the infrared bulbs. To maintain an even temperature in the sugar, turn the sugar over on the fabric work rack every 60 seconds. The peppermint-flavored sugar is used only as the core of the candycanes. Using a four-bulb heating system, it will take approximately 15 minutes to prepare the sugar used for the core of the candycanes.

2. Using the first mass production recommendation and the procedures described in chapter 3, separately but simultaneously fully aerate two 10-inch disks or the equivalent of precooked sugar. Color one of the sugar masses by adding a little red food coloring and maintain a white-colored sugar in the other sugar mass. When the sugars are fully aerated, separately form each piece into the rectangular building shape. Place them on the side of the fabric work rack (without allowing the sugars to touch), together with the peppermint-flavored sugar, under the heat of the single infrared bulb. To maintain an even temperature in the sugar, turn the sugar over on the fabric work rack every 60 seconds. The unflavored red and white sugar is formed into strips and attached around the sides of the peppermint-flavored center. Using a three-bulb heating system, it will take approximately 15 minutes to prepare the unflavored red and white sugar.

ASSEMBLING THE SUGAR

1. Place the peppermint-flavored sugar rectangle at the center of the fabric work rack under the infrared heat. Gradually build the sugar to the blowing-ready temperature and form it into a cylinder approximately 8 inches long and 3 inches in diameter. Return the cylinder to the side of the fabric work rack under the heat of a single infrared bulb, and place the red and white sugar rectangles, without touching, at the center of the fabric work rack under the infrared heat. To maintain an even temperature in the sugar cylinder, turn the cylinder over on the fabric work rack every 60 seconds. Periodically, use your hands to maintain the sugar's cylindrical shape. Using a three-bulb heating system, it will take approximately 6 minutes to prepare the peppermint-flavored sugar into a cylinder.

2. Turn the red and white sugar rectangles over on the fabric work rack every 60 seconds until the sugars reach the pulling-ready temperature. While cutting the rectangles vertically, divide each of the rectangles into three equal parts with scissors. Using scissors, divide one part from each of the rectangles in half along the vertical center, and separately form the four halves into uniformly thick strips ¾ inch wide and 8 inches long. Separately form the four parts from the original rectangles into uniformly thick strips approximately 1½ inches wide and 8 inches long. Place all of the strips, without touching, at the center of the fabric work rack under the infrared heat.

3. Heat the strips until a high-gloss shine covers their surfaces completely. Turn off all of the infrared bulbs and place the sugar cylinder at the front of the fabric work rack. One at a time, carefully attach the high-gloss surface of the strips horizontally around the sides of the sugar cylinder, creating a striped pattern. Start the striped pattern by attaching a ¾-inch-wide red strip to the cylinder (fig. 15–1). Then attach a 1½-inch-wide white strip, 1½-inch-wide red strip, and a

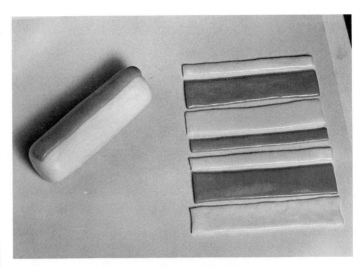

15-1. Attach the ¾-inch-wide red strip to the sugar cylinder.

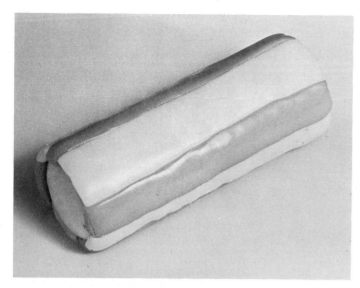

15-2. Attach the strips in a striped pattern along the side of the sugar cylinder.

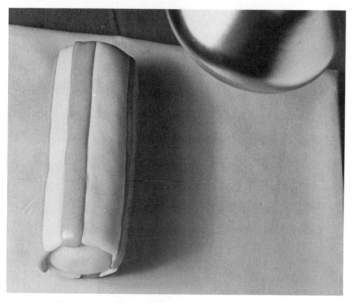

15-3. Place the striped cylinder at one end of the canvas.

¾-inch-wide white strip. Attach the remaining four strips, repeating the same pattern, until the strips have covered the sides of the sugar cylinder completely (fig. 15–2). Make sure the side edges of the strips are connected firmly.

4. Turn on all four infrared bulbs and place the striped cylinder at the center of the fabric work rack under the heat. Remove all the creases on the surface of the sugar by systematically heating the surface of the sugar and then turning the heated surface against the fabric work rack.

PULLING PROCESS

1. Cover a tabletop with a strip of canvas approximately 14 inches wide and 4 feet long. I usually use a number ten duck canvas. Carefully place the sugar cylinder at one end of the canvas strip and position one of the infrared bulbs over the sugar, but do not turn on the bulb (fig. 15–3). Allow the sugar cylinder to cool by turning it in place on the canvas every 60 seconds until the surface of the sugar cylinder is firm, which, depending on the temperature of the sugar when you start to cool the cylinder, can take up to ten minutes. Carefully use your hands to maintain the cylindrical shape while the sugar is cooling.

2. When the surface of the sugar is uniformly firm, turn on the infrared bulb positioned over the sugar cylinder. Carefully form the end of the sugar cylinder facing the open canvas into a uniform cord, 3 inches long and 1½ inches in diameter (fig. 15–3). While slowly and evenly pulling from either end of the cord, pull the point into a cord approximately 18 inches long and ½ inch thick, at the same time gently twisting the cord to create the candycane's familiar swirled stripe. Continue to twist gently while slowly and evenly pulling the cord until it is approximately 36 inches long and ¼ inch thick (fig. 15–4). Remove four 8-inch lengths of cord with scissors and shape each piece into the candycane's familiar hook by carefully curving the last 2 inches at one

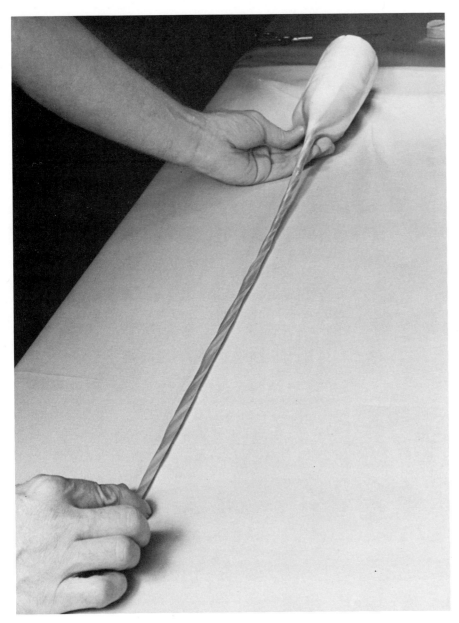

15-5. Curve the end of the cord to create the familiar candycane shape.

15-4. Slowly pull while gently twisting the cord.

end of the cord (fig. 15–5). As the candycanes are shaped, allow them to cool by placing them on a lightly oiled baking sheet.

3. To maintain an even temperature in the sugar cylinder while completing the candycane's pulling process, turn the sugar over in place on the canvas every 2 minutes. Stop periodically during the candycane-pulling process to use your hands to maintain the sugar's cylindrical shape. Repeat the same procedures until all of the sugar cylinder is pulled into candycanes. This volume of sugar will make approximately eighty 8-inch-long and ¼-inch-thick hooked candycanes.

PART 5

BLOWN- AND PULLED-SUGAR CANDY

CHAPTER 16

SPECIALTY CANDIES

The sugar-blowing and sugar-pulling procedures used in this book can be used to create a wide variety of unique confections. This chapter will provide the procedures used to make two types of candy: a small sugar-blown strawberry filled with a chocolate and liqueur center, and hickory nuts individually coated with grape-flavored pulled sugar, assembled to look like a bunch of natural grapes.

BLOWN-SUGAR STRAWBERRY CANDY

1. Using the procedures described in chapter 3, fully aerate a 4-inch disk of strawberry-flavored pre-cooked sugar. Color the sugar by adding a little red and orange food coloring, using a ratio of three parts red to one part orange. When the sugar is fully aerated, form it into a tight mass and place it at the back of the fabric work rack under the heat of a single infrared bulb. Position the remaining three infrared bulbs over the center of the fabric work rack. Maintain an even temperature in the sugar mass by periodically folding the hotter surface sugar into the center. Using a four-bulb heating system, it will take approximately 6 minutes to fully aerate the sugar.

2. Using scissors, remove a circular piece of sugar approximately ¼ inch in diameter from the sugar mass. Form the piece of sugar into the rectangular building shape and place it at the center of the

fabric work rack under the infrared heat. Gradually build the sugar into a blowing-ready ball.

3. Attach the blowpipe to the sugar. I usually use a 6-millimeter blowpipe to make the strawberry candies.

4. Using the procedures described in the blowing process of the sphere, blow softly while rotating the blowpipe and sugar evenly until the air chamber has filled two-thirds of the ball. With your fingertips, gently pull the last half of the ball into a soft point, and carefully pull the ball away from the end of the blowpipe to create a margin between the end of the blowpipe and the start of the blown piece. It will take approximately 1½ minutes to complete this step.

5. Maintain the strawberry's tapered end by using your fingers to restrict the outward expansion of the pointed end of the sphere while blowing. Continue to rotate and blow softly until the air chamber has penetrated through to the point, and the sugar has expanded to a strawberry approximately ½ inch in diameter at the top, and ½ inch long, tapering to a point at the bottom. It will take approximately 1½ minutes to finish blowing the strawberry.

6. Using the procedures described in the cooling process, allow the strawberry to cool in front of a fan set on high.

16-1. Carefully pipe chocolate into the strawberry.

7. Remove the blowpipe from the sugar and place the strawberry on a fabric work rack away from the heat. Be sure to leave a hole, approximately $3/16$ inch in diameter, at the top of the strawberry. If necessary, heat the top of the strawberry over the flame of an alcohol burner and carefully use the point of a paring knife or a toothpick to flare a hole at the top of the strawberry.

   Repeat the blowing process procedures until all of the sugar mass has been blown into small strawberries. A 5-inch disk will make twenty small strawberries.

CHOCOLATE AND LIQUEUR FILLING

1. Using a small double-boiler saucepan, slowly melt approximately $1/3$ pound of semisweet dark chocolate. When the chocolate is completely melted, remove the top of the double-boiler with the chocolate from the heat. Allow the chocolate to cool for 10 minutes.

2. Lightly oil the chambers of a plastic, miniature-cube ice-cube tray and place the strawberries into the cube chambers. Using a spoon, place the melted chocolate into a small pastry paper cone, a small cloth, or a plastic pastry bag with a small tip. Carefully pipe the chocolate into the hole at the top of the strawberries until the chocolate is approximately $1/8$ inch below the top edge of the strawberry (fig. 16–1).

3. Place the tray of strawberries into a plastic, zipper-lock freezer bag along with some Humi-sorb. Place the bag into a freezer for approximately 15 minutes to allow the chocolate to partially harden. Do not put the strawberries into the freezer uncovered.

4. After 15 minutes, remove the bag from the freezer and remove the tray of strawberries from the bag. Using the small solid-glass manipulator, carefully make an indentation approximately $1/4$ inch deep and $3/16$ inch in diameter into the chocolate inside the strawberries by gently pushing and turning the glass rod into the chocolate (fig. 16–2).

5. Using a small glass eyedropper, add 4 drops of liqueur into the indentation in the chocolate. I usually use a strawberry or raspberry liqueur for the strawberry candies.

6. Seal the liqueur in the chocolate by carefully piping chocolate into the strawberries until they are filled with chocolate. Again place the tray of strawberries into a freezer bag with Humi-sorb and allow the chocolate to harden in the freezer for approximately 10 minutes.

FINISHING THE STRAWBERRY

1. Using the procedures described in chapter 3, fully aerate a 5-inch disk of strawberry-flavored precooked sugar. (The procedure used to flavor the sugar is described in step 5 of the *Cooking Process* in chapter 2.) Color the sugar by adding a small amount of green food coloring. When the sugar is fully aerated, form the sugar into the rectangular building shape and place it on the fabric work rack away from the heat. Allow the sugar to cool to the pulling-ready temperature. Turn the sugar every 60 seconds to maintain a uniform temperature while cooling.

2. Pull the required number of strawberry leaves, each approximately ¼ inch long and ⅛ inch wide. I usually use four leaves per strawberry. As the leaves are completed, place them on the fabric work rack away from the heat.

3. Using scissors, remove a circular piece of green sugar approximately ⅛ inch in diameter. Press the ball with your fingertips into a flat circle approximately ¼ inch in diameter. The flat circle is used to cover the hole at the top of the strawberry. Using the same procedures, make the required number of flat circle strawberry tops.

4. Using scissors, remove a circular piece of green sugar approximately ½ inch in diameter. Slowly and evenly pull the ball into a uniform cord 8 inches long and ¹⁄₁₆ inch thick. Remove the required amount of ³⁄₁₆-inch lengths of cord with scissors. These pieces are used to create the strawberry's stem.

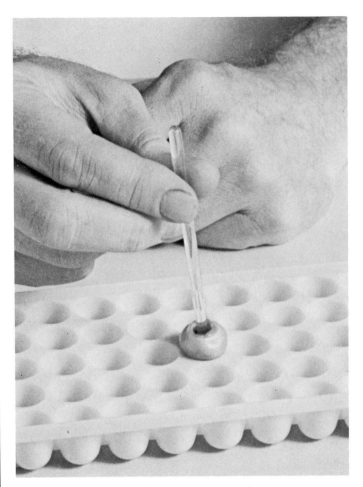

16-2. Gently make an indentation into the chocolate.

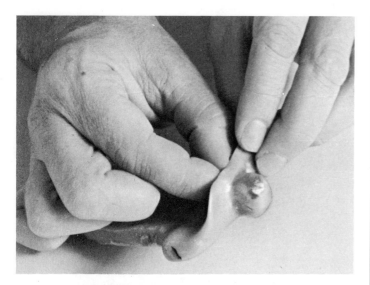

16-3. Push the hickory nut into the sugar.

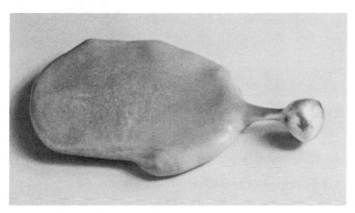

16-4. Pull the nut through the sugar and pinch the sugar at the back of the nut into a thin cord.

5. Heat the edge of the flat circle of green sugar over the flame of an alcohol burner and attach it over the hole at the top of the strawberry. Make sure the green sugar completely seals the hole. If necessary, quickly heat the top of the strawberry over the alcohol burner and use your finger to press the edge of the green sugar to the top of the strawberry.

6. Individually heat the stem end of the strawberry leaves and the strawberry stems over the alcohol burner and attach them to the top of the strawberry (C-22).

PULLED-SUGAR-COATED HICKORY NUTS

Hickory nuts were chosen for this chapter, although any similar sized nut can be used. I sometimes substitute raisins for the hickory nuts.

1. Using the procedures described in chapter 3, fully aerate a 5-inch disk of grape-flavored precooked sugar. Color the sugar purple by adding equal amounts of red and blue food coloring. When the sugar is fully aerated, form it into the rectangular building shape and place it on the fabric work rack away from the heat. Allow the sugar to cool to the pulling-ready temperature. Turn the sugar every 60 seconds to maintain a uniform temperature while cooling.

2. Spread the edge of the sugar into a thin band. Push a hickory nut halfway into the thin sugar approximately ¾ inch below the edge of the band (fig. 16–3). While using one hand to push the nut into the band, use your other hand to pull the nut through the bottom of the band. Pinch the sugar down, creating a thin cord at the back of the nut (fig. 16–4). Remove the nut with scissors, leaving approximately ¼ inch of cord at the back of the nut. Using the same procedures, pass approximately thirty hickory nuts through the sugar.

3. Individually heat the ends of the cords over the flame of an alcohol burner and attach the nuts so they resemble a bunch of natural grapes (fig. 16–5).

4. Using scissors, remove a circular piece of sugar approximately ½ inch in diameter. Slowly and evenly pull the ball into a uniform cord approximately ⅛ inch thick. Remove a 1½-inch length of cord with scissors and slightly curve the cord. The small cord is used to create the stem for the imitation grape bunch. Heat the end of the stem over an alcohol burner and attach it to the front of the grapes (C-22).

16-5. Attach the sugar-coated nuts to resemble a bunch of natural grapes.

SUGAR-STUDIO EQUIPMENT

The hot-wire cutter can be purchased from:
Sugar Systems
4011 West Fountain
Brown Deer, WI 53209

Inquiries about purchasing all other sugar-studio
equipment should be sent to:
Peter Boyle
608 Ridgemont
Rochester, NY 14626

To find a local distributor for the Staley 4400
Sweetose corn syrup, write to:
A. E. Staley
P.O. Box 151
Decatur, IL 62525

INDEX